Choices and Challenges

Choices and Challenges

■ ■ ■

Charter School
Performance
in Perspective

PRISCILLA WOHLSTETTER
JOANNA SMITH
CAITLIN C. FARRELL

Harvard Education Press
Cambridge, Massachusetts

KH

Library of Congress Control Number 2012951728

Paperback ISBN 978-1-61250-541-1
Library Edition ISBN 978-1-61250-542-8

Published by Harvard Education Press,
an imprint of the Harvard Education Publishing Group

Harvard Education Press
8 Story Street
Cambridge, MA 02138

Cover Design: Deborah Hodgdon
Cover Photo: Digital Vision/Getty Images

The typefaces used in this book are Sabon and Ocean Sans.

10/20/14

We dedicate this book
to all of the experimentalists
in public education
who are testing out new ways
of restructuring classrooms,
schools, and school districts.

CONTENTS

FOREWORD

FOR DECADES, research on charter schools has been characterized by conflicting studies, arguments about appropriate methods, and high-profile bickering in the media.[1] The research controversy is fueled by deep-seated ideologies, differing opinions concerning the nature of public education, lots of money supporting both sides, and the inherent complexity of assessing education success. Charges and countercharges about research findings evolve into what Jeffrey Henig calls a "spin cycle" of media rollout.[2] The casual observer does not know what to make of all this disputation.

As president of the California State Board of Education, I make decisions about charter schools every month. About one-third of our agenda concerns charter schools. Until now, I have not been able to bring an organized and coherent set of charter research findings to my work. In *Choices and Challenges: Charter School Performance in Perspective*, Priscilla Wohlstetter and her colleagues set out to fill this gap.

This book provides clarity and balance to much of the contested terrain of charter research. It begins with a concise overview of the historical roots and initial stage of the charter movement, highlights the goals initially set for the movement by authorizing legislation, and traces the increasing sophistication of charter school research in interrogating the movement's success.[3] While the scope includes getting inside the "black box" of charter schools and classrooms, the discussion transcends the usual dueling studies focused on student achievement that dominate popular media.[4] Charters have many goals beyond increasing student achievement, so the authors include multiple dimensions of charter operations and impact. They include a "retrospective synthesis" of over five hundred academic publications encompassing more than a decade.

One of the book's most important contributions is to specify what we *do not* know about charters, as well as the central findings emerging from the research base. The writers proceed with humility and show a fine grasp of the data and methodological limitations. The major problem the book confronts is the limitations of the research base. Much of it consists of individual case studies or includes nonrepresentative samples. As the authors note, "the preponderance of research on charter schools is fairly limited in scope."

The achievement literature is synthesized in a single chapter. The authors provide a road map to navigate the complexity and confusion surrounding this issue, but at the end they acknowledge, as Julian Betts and Emily Tang put it, "that the majority of charter school studies take snapshots of student achievement at one point in time, or compare successive cohorts of students in a given grade." They highlight the absence of large-scale random control studies that are the "gold standard" for some types of education topics.

Several of the chapters integrate existing qualitative and quantitative studies about a specific topic. This is very useful for examining issues such as teacher quality in charter schools and the competitive impact of charters upon non-charter public schools. As the authors show, the preponderance of evidence undercuts the allegation that charter selection "creams" high performing students and underrepresents low-income and minority students in cities.

Even where there are data limitations, the book provides a clear guide to the crucial underlying issues and data needed for definitive conclusions. This is evident in the accountability chapter, where the various types of potential accountability approaches are clearly delineated.

One chapter examines the alleged unintended consequences of charters, such as increasing segregation, and the impact of charter management organizations. The evidence concerning segregation is mixed, but the authors caution that some charters are designed to meet the needs of specific types of students, so a diverse student body is not likely.

A theme that emerges throughout the book is the underlying story of charter maturation, persistence, and change. The authors enlist this perspective to help interpret the evolving and expanding research base. Early charter research focused upon the desirability of charter school creation, support, and growth. More recent research has increased in sophistication and has begun to address the quality and impact of the 5,600 charter schools in forty-one states and the District of Columbia. Through their review, the authors trace the evolution of charter school research over more than a decade.

In focusing on the performance of charter schools relative to the goals initially set for them, the authors also acknowledge the impact of state and local politics on the discourse surrounding charter schools.[5] Charter politics are diverse and complex depending on state and local contexts and on particular types of charters (e.g., for-profit vs. nonprofit). Charter politics in Georgia are very different from charter politics in Arizona. Nonetheless, both the research and the perspectives shared by the diverse array of commentators in one of the final chapters indicate that charters are no passing fad—they are here to stay, and they promise to have a lasting, if varied, impact on the educational landscape.

The research synthesis presented in this volume is clearly written, concise, and comprehensible. *Choices and Challenges* serves a broad audience—scholars, practitioners, and the general public—that follows education issues. It offers valuable guidance for policy makers concerning charter issues but does not presume to recommend what decisions should be made. I know I will find it an invaluable resource in my role as a state official.

> —Michael W. Kirst
> *Professor Emeritus of Education*
> *and Business Administration,*
> *Stanford University, and President,*
> *California State Board of Education*

INTRODUCTION

THE LAUNCH OF THE CHARTER SCHOOL movement in 1991 galvanized Democrats and Republicans, liberals and conservatives, to support an ambitious effort to restructure public education. Charter schools offered opportunities for educators, parents, and community organizations to enter the education sector to create, reform, and operate public schools. Taking stock more than twenty years later, studies show that student enrollment in charter schools more than quadrupled during the first decade of the twenty-first century, from 340,000 to 1.6 million students.[1] More than five hundred new charter schools were opened in 2011–2012, enrolling more than 200,000 additional students, representing a 13 percent increase over the previous year. As seen in figure I.1, by the 2011–2012 school year, over 5,600 charter schools in forty-one states plus the District of Columbia were serving more than two million students.[2]

While charter schools won early support from both sides of the political aisle, they were initially considered something of a fringe movement. In recent years, charter schools have emerged as integral to many urban districts' reform strategies.[3] More generally, federal and state policy makers have institutionalized charters by intentionally including them in federal turnaround models (e.g., School Improvement Grants and the No Child Left Behind Act) and by setting up new federal programs to assist in their scale-up and expansion. So while charter schools certainly have not lacked controversy over the years, proponents and detractors alike admit that they are here to stay—a permanent reform that will be tinkered with but that likely will not disappear. The 2011 Phi Delta

FIGURE I.1

Growth of charter schools in the U.S.

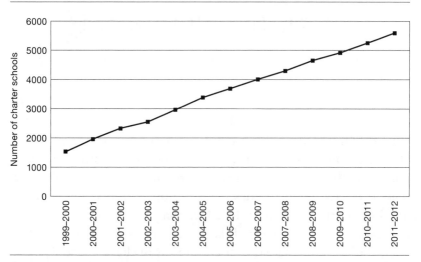

Source: National Alliance for Public Charter Schools, "The Public Charter Schools Dashboard" (Washington, DC:2012).

Kappa/Gallup poll recorded a 70 percent public approval rating for charter schools, its highest ever.[4]

Charter schools are a unique breed—part of the public education system, open to all students tuition-free, and yet unburdened from many of the rules and regulations that govern and sometimes constrain district-run public schools. Each charter school operates within the detailed framework of its own performance contract or "charter," agreed upon between the charter authorizer and the school. Collectively, charter schools were intended to diversify the providers of public education; to encourage and incubate innovations with regard to education programs, school governance, staffing, and budgeting; and to improve student achievement. In addition, charter schools were expected to broaden public school choice and to serve as models for improving teaching and learning in district-run public schools.

In the beginning, charter schools were either existing public schools that converted to charter status or new schools started from scratch by teachers, parents, and/or community organizations to fill a particular market niche, such as educating at-risk, special education, or English-learner populations.[5] Most charter schools were smaller than district-run schools, and nearly all were site-based; the vast majority were elementary schools. Over the years, charter schools have diversified. In the 2009–2010 school year, secondary and combined (e.g., K–8 or 6–12) schools accounted for 27 percent and 19 percent of charter schools, respectively.[6] Service delivery increasingly includes hybrid models and cyber charters.[7]

With the charter school movement entering its third decade, we have little cumulative knowledge about the performance of the chartering sector as a whole. Have charter schools succeeded in certain areas? Where have they fallen short? Equally important, what factors and influences help explain charter school outcomes?

As observers and participants in education reform know first-hand, the pure quantity of research on charter schools over the past two decades since the reform was introduced in the United States is astounding. In this book, we offer a retrospective synthesis of the research on charter schools. We selected more than five hundred academic publications and then coded, analyzed, and synthesized the findings (as explained in the appendix, Notes on Research). Our intent was to evaluate charter schools by their legislative goals to help inform policies and practices moving forward for all public schools—charter and non-charter public schools alike.

In this introductory chapter, we offer an overview of the evolution of the charter school movement, from its origins through successive generations of implementation. Next, we describe the diversity of goals set forth in charter school laws to lay the foundation for interpreting the findings in the chapters that follow, arranged by the array of legislated goals of charter schools.

A BRIEF CHRONOLOGY OF THE CHARTER SCHOOL MOVEMENT— WAVES OF REFORM

The Origins

Charter schools are an education reform imported from Britain. Many of the first articles about charter schools in the United States considered the question of what U.S. charter schools could learn from Britain's grant-maintained schools.[8] The development of grant-maintained schools was spurred in the U.K. by a government foundation that encouraged schools with additional funding and technical assistance to take on decision-making responsibilities over the education program, the budget, and staffing.

In the United States, the 1980s was a time of considerable experimentation with individual education reforms. The charter movement was the latest in a series of reforms that were ultimately bundled into a package that became charter schools. In the 1980s, school districts across the country experimented with school-based management, an idea borrowed from the private sector on the assumption that when decision making was decentralized to school sites, school communities would make smart decisions tailored to the needs of their unique communities, thus strengthening the commitment to the reform agenda.[9] Under school-based management, school communities were empowered to make the same kind of decisions over the school's education program, budget, and staff as in Britain's grant-maintained schools.

Other experiments of the 1980s explored deregulation—loosening state education codes and the rules and regulations governing schools—so that individual schools would have more discretion in making decisions. Research in this area assessed the value of blanket waivers as compared to waivers that were awarded piecemeal, provision by provision.[10] The common conclusion was that blanket waivers were far more liberating to schools and also resulted in school improvements far more rapidly.

Finally, there were reforms that emphasized school choice. While school choice in the modern era of public schooling had been linked to magnet schools for desegregation purposes, the new wave of choice reforms pioneered in Minnesota with the passage of the first charter school law in 1991 added a different dimension. State and district tuition dollars would follow the child to the school of his or her choice, adding competition to local school systems with clear winners and losers.[11] Preceding the adoption of charters in Minnesota, the state had experimented with school choice at many different points in time, the most recent being the Post-Secondary Education Options (PSEO) law that allowed junior and senior high school students to enroll in college, earning credits simultaneously toward high school and college graduations. The PSEO program, championed by Republican state legislator Connie Levi, borrowed from Milton Friedman's voucher idea, but limited choice to only the public sector and to students in high school.[12] As with vouchers, tuition dollars followed the student.

At the same time states were experimenting with these reforms, the Reagan administration's National Commission on Excellence in Education released its report titled "A Nation at Risk," concluding that U.S. schools were failing. This report touched off a wave of efforts to restructure education. The national discussion about restructuring eventually brought together the ideas of Ray Budde, an educator and administrator in Massachusetts, with those of Albert Shanker, president of the American Federation of Teachers. Ray Budde had a strong interest in "the way things are organized" and in "how things work or don't work in organizations." His paper entitled "Education by Charter," written back in the mid-1970s, offered ideas for the reorganization of school districts.[13] Subsequently Budde had his paper published by Northeast Regional Lab in 1988, and it was disseminated widely.[14] It eventually got into the hands of Al Shanker, who had a weekly column in the *New York Times*. In one of his columns during July 1988, Shanker discussed a speech he had recently given at the National Press Club supporting the idea of teachers setting up autonomous schools within schools. Shanker mentioned that Ray Budde had the best name for these schools: charter schools. Shanker also expanded on Budde's idea by proposing that teachers ought to be able to start new schools outside an existing school building.[15]

The final key actor in this tale of the charter movement was Minnesota's Citizens League, whose members served as policy champions. Early on, the Citizens League endorsed parental choice. Further, the League recommended that low-income students should have the choice to attend both public and non-public schools, and they welcomed the idea of creating *new* schools in the public sector. Aside from school choice, the Citizens League supported the idea of decentralizing decision making to individual schools; in 1987 it proposed "cooperatively managed schools" and endorsed the idea of giving teachers larger professional roles.

By the late 1980s the Citizens League was ready to act. It released a new report that bundled all of the ideas its members supported into a document titled "Chartered Schools = Choices for Educators + Quality for All Students." The next stop was the Minnesota state legislature. The politics in the state were just right, with the strong Democratic-Farmer-Labor Party arguing the values of populism, deregulation, and decentralization right along with the Republican governor Arne Carlson, who pushed the public school choice initiatives advanced by his Democratic predecessor, Rudy Perpich. In addition, the policy champions of the charter movement (including Ted Kolderie and Joe Nathan of the Citizens League) and state legislators (Senator Ember Reichgott Junge and Representative Ken Nelson) were waiting to seize the window of opportunity. After several failed attempts, Governor Perpich, together with Tom Nelson, the lobbyist for the Minnesota Education Association whom the governor had just appointed as his new commissioner of education, lent their lobbying muscle, and in 1991 the new governor, Arne Carlson, signed the bill into law.[16] The bill passed the Minnesota legislature by a margin of eighty-five to forty-five in the House and fifty-six to eleven in the Senate, and the nation's first two charter schools opened the next year, both still operating today.[17] California followed suit with charter legislation in 1992, and its first charter schools opened the following year.[18] And so the charter school movement was born.

First Generation—the Era of "Let All Flowers Bloom"

As indicated above, charter schooling in the United States was a reform enacted by individual state legislatures, and so the context of charter schooling rested largely with the politics of the varied state and local jurisdictions. In California, for instance, the adoption of the charter school law came about because a referendum was placed on the ballot in November 1992 for a statewide voucher initiative, which was supported by the business community but vehemently opposed by the teacher unions.[19] The charter school bill was introduced quickly into the legislature as a benign alternative to vouchers, and with the support of the powerful teacher unions, the California charter law was enacted in 1992.

In contrast, as described earlier, Minnesota's charter schools were the result of a natural progression in the state's long tradition of public school choice, welcomed by the Citizens League, the Minnesota state legislature, and two successive governors.[20] Furthermore, key principles of the charter movement—decentralization, choice, and professional opportunities for teachers—had been pushed by the Citizens League in the years leading up to the bill's introduction.

With the first generation of charter schools beginning in the early 1990s and continuing through most of the decade, attention was focused on the states—the pace at which charter laws were being adopted, the difference in content across laws, and whether or not charters were a passing fad to be replaced by the next reform de jour. During this decade the number of states enacting charter laws grew exponentially, from one in 1991 to twenty-five by 1998. States experimented with the length of the charter term and with who the authorizers should be. Most state laws authorized charter schools for three to five years, but Arizona, at the extreme, offered fifteen-year charters. The question of who would serve as authorizers of charter schools was likewise varied. Some states empowered local school districts to authorize charters, other states set up special-purpose charter school boards; a few empowered state universities, and still others adopted a combination.[21] Experimentation was key during this generation.

Also during the first generation there was an ongoing discussion of what charter schools were supposed to be. Were they to be considered nonprofits, public organizations, or some hybrid of the two? What types of schools were opening, and who was founding them, teaching in them, funding them, and enrolling in them? California had internal disputes about how much autonomy charter schools should be given and ended up with a two-class system: first, independent charters that had control over the education program, personnel, and budget; and second, dependent charters, or what Vanourek, Manno, and Finn referred to as "faux" charters, which were dependent on the district for approval of all financial decisions.[22]

The first charter schools were either started from scratch by teachers, parents, and/or community organizations, or, when allowed by state law, were district schools that converted to charter status, as in California. Referred to as "mom and pops," "one-offs," or "stand-alones," the first generation of charter schools were mostly targeted at students who had not been well served by traditional public schools. Early charter schools established specialized curricula to appeal to at-risk high school students who were over age, to special education students, and to English-learner students whose parents were recent immigrants. Personalization and preparing students for the twenty-first century were common mantras.[23]

Toward the end of the decade, the need for a national professional association for the charter community emerged. In the early years, the national charter organization operated under the aegis of the Center for Education Reform in Washington, DC, led by the venerable Jeanne Allen, a community and political advocate for all forms of public school choice, especially charter schools. In 2005, the National Alliance for Public Charter Schools was created, spurred by state charter associations that felt the need for a more expansive structure that spanned all states with charter school legislation. Among the state organizations pushing for a national association were CANEC (California Network of Educational Charters, now known as California Charter Schools Association) and the Massachusetts Charter School Resource Center in Boston.

Second Generation—the Expansion Era

By September 1999, more than 1,400 charter schools existed in thirty-two states and the District of Columbia, with four additional states having charter statutes but no charter schools yet open.[24]

During this period, with the enactment of the Public Charter Schools Program in 1995, Congress carved out a role for the federal government with respect to charters. As designed, the program encouraged state educational agencies to apply for funds, which could then be disseminated to charter schools in their states. The U.S. Department of Education left it up to the states to decide how to disperse the funds. However, it stipulated that the money should be used to plan, design, and implement new charter schools, as well as to disseminate information on successful charter schools.

A loose network of state technical assistance centers also assisted expansion of charter schools. In response to England's Grant-Maintained Schools Foundation—a government group whose purpose was to accelerate the development and launch of autonomous schools throughout the country—Eric Premack, founding director of the Charter Schools Development Center in Sacramento, California, closely followed by Linda Brown, creator of the Massachusetts Charter School Resource Center in Boston, pioneered the first such centers to offer technical assistance to people interested in starting charter schools. During the late 1990s and into the early twenty-first century, these technical assistance centers sprang up in nearly every state that passed a charter law. The centers were often in addition to a state's professional charter school association, which typically focused more on advocacy work and membership services to the charter community.

In terms of research, this wave of the charter school movement, in the late 1990s and into the early twenty-first century, sought to answer questions of accountability, autonomy, and the spillover effects of charters on district reform. Were charter schools fulfilling the goal of providing "lighthouses" of innovation, or were they more akin to "islands"? Had they exchanged autonomy for accountability, or was it a free-for-all in which the mantra of the first wave of charter schools, "Let all flowers bloom," ruled the day? This brought to the fore discussions about charter authorizers. Were multiple types of authorizers in a state better than one type of authorizer? And more to the point, were school districts as authorizers inherently in conflict with charters? Should they be relieved of their authorizing responsibilities? The National Association of Charter Authorizers was founded in 2000 with the express purpose of identifying promising authorizing practices and scaling them up across state boundaries.

Over time, the kind of charter schools started by groups of disgruntled parents or teachers began to morph into something else. First, for-profit companies entered the scene, hoping to take advantage of economies of scale. These education management organizations (EMOs) were prevented by provisions in charter school laws in many states from opening charter schools themselves, but they gained a presence by partnering with charter schools to deliver a menu of services from curriculum to back office support. On the heels of EMOs, a nonprofit version of school networks known as charter management organizations (CMOs) emerged. CMOs tend to embrace a particular educational philosophy or aim to serve a specific student population or geographic area. They usually have home offices where many administrative, operational, and instructional duties are centralized to help member schools focus on instruction.[25] The philanthropic community, interested in systemic reform and bringing charters to scale, invested in charter operators who intended to scale up. With funding from foundations such as NewSchools Venture Fund and the Walton Family Foundation, and later the Charter School Growth Fund, CMOs began to proliferate.

As studies started to assess the student achievement outcomes of charter schools, the emerging question was, against whose performance should charter school outcomes be compared? Early studies of charter school outcomes looked at the results of charter schools at a single point in time. Researchers used state end-of-grade tests, for example, and often compared these results with state or district averages. Findings from studies of this type raised objections that charter school students were somehow different from the "average" district or state student, making comparisons difficult, but the more valid question was, different in what ways? Another wave of studies tried to get at the question of whether charter schools "skimmed" the brightest students from non-charter public schools or whether charter schools tended to serve the most disadvantaged students. The extent to which charter schools served special education students or whether they were being screened out also emerged over the years as a prevalent area of study.

Analytic techniques for examining trends in student outcomes became more sophisticated in the second generation, with the use of longitudinal student-level panel data to assess value-added and, in some cases, experimental designs afforded by the random assignment of students through charter school lotteries (see chapter 3). As research methods grew more sophisticated, mixed results continued to make it difficult to know what differentiated high achieving charter schools from those whose performance was indistinguishable from or lower than non-charter public schools.

Third Generation—the Era of Refinements

The third generation can be described as the era of refinements, both in state laws and in authorizing practices. For example, charter school laws differ significantly across the states, which strongly influences both the number of charter schools and how they operate in different locales. More than half the states with charter school statutes have limited the number of charter schools allowed in the state. Some states (e.g., Alaska, Arkansas, Mississippi) have absolute caps on the number of charter schools, while others (e.g., California, the District of Columbia, Idaho) have caps that are raised annually as designated by statute, allowing some number of additional schools each year. Still others restrict the number of students per school (e.g., Connecticut), the types of charter schools or authorizers (e.g., Hawaii, Massachusetts, New York), or the location of charter schools (e.g., Illinois, North Carolina, Oklahoma).[26]

However, in recent months, several state legislatures have begun to reexamine caps. In particular, Louisiana eliminated its cap, Delaware let a one-year moratorium on new charter schools lapse, and Illinois and Tennessee raised the number of charter schools allowed under their caps.[27] This relaxing of caps on the number of charter schools is due, at least partially, to support for charter schools by President Obama and Secretary of Education Arne Duncan, including specified funding priorities in the department's Race to the Top fund that favored states with unrestricted charter laws.[28] The federal push may also explain the recent surge in charter school enrollment.

During the third generation of charter schools, post-2006 or so, public sentiment shifted away from "will charter schools survive?" to "they will persist, so how can quality be improved?" In this generation of charter schools, we have the promulgation of model charter laws and standards for high-quality authorizing, both initiatives led by national charter school associations—the National Alliance for Public Charter Schools and the National Association of Charter School Authorizers. Also important to note in recent years is the institutionalization of charter schools as an integral piece of the education landscape, attracting federal and state dollars for expansion and turning around chronically low performing schools.

In the early years of the charter school movement, one of the policy champions, Ted Kolderie of Minnesota's Citizens League and now of Education|Evolving in Minneapolis, created and circulated an informal document that laid out the contents for a model charter law.[29] At the time, Kolderie wanted to develop a tool to assist state policy makers across the United States in drafting credible charter school legislation. In this third generation of the movement, the idea of a model charter law has reemerged, only this time with an eye toward "strengthening" the charter laws that already have been enacted. In 2010 the National Alliance for Public Charter Schools launched the "Measuring Up" project, which evaluates how existing state charter laws measure up to a model law they created. Among the components of the model law are provisions that enable innovation, promote transparency about how charter schools perform and how they are held accountable, and provide fair access to public funds and facilities. The Alliance compares each state charter law to the model law and offers numerical rankings on how the law stacks up, in effect helping state policy makers recognize where their charter laws are strong and where refinements could be made.[30]

With this latest generation of charter schools, a renewed scrutiny of the groups that approve, oversee, and renew charter school petitions—the authorizers—has also emerged, raising new questions about their role and responsibility in ensuring a high-quality charter sector. What are the policies and practices of authorizers that lead to the operation of high-quality charter schools? What is the role of authorizers in enabling the replication of charter models that work, while closing down charters that do not? Spearheading this effort is the National Association of Charter School Authorizers (NACSA). Under the leadership of Greg Richmond, NACSA has emphasized the importance of having authorizers conduct rigorous oversight of the charter schools they authorize and of holding discussions with a broad set of stakeholders including: authorizers, such as school districts, that had chartering responsibilities foisted on them and needed guidance in how to do the work; charter operators who wanted to see "bad" charters closed down; and policy makers who wanted the autonomy-for-accountability mantra of the charter movement strengthened. NACSA's "Principles and Standards for Quality Charter School Authorizing," first released in 2004 and revised in 2010, offers standards and practical guidance in developing authorizer capacity with regard to: 1) the charter application and decision-making processes, 2) oversight and evaluation of charter schools, and 3) revocation and renewal decision making.[31] More recently, NACSA created the Fund for Authorizing Excellence, which awards competitive grants to authorizers to assist with improving quality in the areas of authorizer evaluation, strategic planning, and implementation.[32] In sum, the focus on charter schools has broadened in the third generation to include the performance of charter authorizers and, increasingly, the relationship between authorizer behavior and charter school quality.

Another feature in this third generation of charters is their institutionalization in the policy landscape. Observers attribute the recent boom in charter schools to the Obama administration's $4-billion Race to the Top competition, which rewarded states for implementing education reforms that encouraged the growth of charter schools. Sixteen states lifted caps on the number of charter schools, and enrollment has soared, according to the National Conference of State Legislatures and the National Alliance for Public Charter Schools.[33] The U.S. Department of Education also expanded the Charter Schools Program to include a separate fund for CMOs: the Grants for Replication and Expansion of High Quality Charter Schools.[34] CMOs were also rewarded through the Obama administration's Investing in Innovation (i3) awards.[35] In August 2010, two CMOs—the national Knowledge is Power Program (KIPP) Foundation and the Alliance for College-Ready Public Schools in Los Angeles—were awarded about $50 million each. The Bill and Melinda Gates Foundation's College-Ready Promise funded four CMOs in Los Angeles, along with several school districts across the country, to improve college-readiness rates for low-income minority students by improving teacher effectiveness.[36] More recently, in 2011, the Broad Foundation announced a second Broad Prize for school systems: the Broad Prize for Public Charter Schools, an annual award of $250,000 to a CMO with notably improved student achievement, which was modeled after the Broad District Prize.[37]

With the explosion of CMOs, research studies have begun to investigate the impact of this network approach.[38] Is there an ideal number of schools for a CMO to create? Do CMOs run the risk of replicating school districts—and the hierarchical structures CMOs sought to combat—if they grow too large? Are CMOs able to improve student achievement and close the achievement gap more reliably and effectively than stand-alone charter schools? Finally, in this generation, we have also observed an increasing focus on the academic programs of charter schools: what's going on inside the "black box" of charter schooling. Thus far, such studies are largely based on case study research with the aim of identifying and disseminating promising practices.

ASSESSING THE ARRAY OF PERFORMANCE GOALS FOR CHARTER SCHOOLS

Judging from the media and the preponderance of research studies focused on student achievement, observers might logically conclude that charter schools have a single goal—to improve student achievement. However, this is not true. From the beginning, charter schools were envisioned by proponents as multipurpose. Yes, they were designed to undertake improvements in schools that would produce higher student achievement or reductions in the achievement gap. However, charter schools were also supported as a policy lever to break up the monopoly of school districts as the sole provider of public education and to push the public system toward change and improvement. As Ted Kolderie reminds us, charter legislation is a platform that enables schools to experiment and try new things. Charter schools are not limited to one type of school. As Kolderie is quoted as saying in an interview, "People want to know whether a charter school is better than a district school, which to me is essentially like asking whether eating out is better than eating at home. It depends. What is it we're eating?"[39]

In this section, we offer a review of the range of goals stated in charter school laws—what the creators of the laws intended for charter schools to accomplish. While there are differences across state laws in the purpose of charter schools related to specific state priorities, there are also commonalities.

In reviewing the stated purposes in charter laws, we identified an array of goals:

- Increase opportunities for teachers
- Increase innovations in education programs
- Increase student performance
- Increase school autonomy
- Increase opportunities for parent involvement
- Increase school accountability
- Increase competition among public schools

FIGURE I.2

Frequency of goals in charter school laws

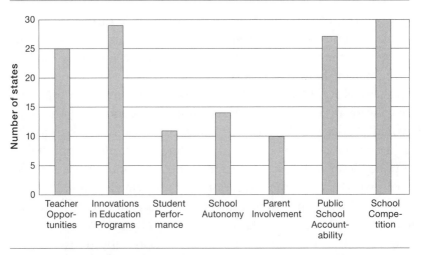

Source: data compiled by reviewing O'Neill and Ziebarth, *Charter School Law Deskbook*, 2008–2009 Edition (Charlottesville, VA: LexisNexis,2009).

Of the forty-one charter school laws on the books, thirty-two include a preamble or purposes section; the review that follows is based on the charter laws with stated goals as found in O'Neill and Ziebarth's 2008–2009 *Charter School Law Deskbook.*[40] These categories were initially borrowed from an unpublished paper by Andy Smarick written for the National Alliance for Public Charter Schools, but they have been further refined and adjusted.[41]

Regarding the popularity of stated purposes, states were most interested in encouraging innovations in academic programs, with 91 percent highlighting this as a purpose in the law. Phrases like "innovative programs" (e.g., Indiana, Texas, Virginia) and "encourage the use of different and innovative teaching methods" (e.g., Colorado, Iowa, Louisiana) appeared most frequently.[42] Charter school laws written prior to and just after the turn of the century were very interested in preparing students for the demands of the twenty-first century. While most did not specify what they meant by that, in practice "prepared" often translated into acquisition of technological skills and an emphasis on globalization—students' awareness of the world around them.

Closely related to charter schools as engines for innovation was the idea of new opportunities for teachers, building upon the earlier experimentation with school-based management. This purpose appeared with a frequency of 78 percent. Laws were enacted to "create new professional opportunities for teachers" (e.g., Colorado, Tennessee, Wyoming), to "give teachers more ownership of their schools" (e.g., Illinois, Florida), to provide "freedom from conventional program constraints and mandates" (e.g., Kansas), and to create "the opportunity to be responsible for the learning program at the school site" (e.g., Idaho, Minnesota, Pennsylvania, South Carolina).[43]

In addition to new opportunities for teachers, charter school laws focused on efforts to increase parent involvement in schools. This purpose emphasized the roles of parents as creators of public schools. Moreover, states specified parent roles in terms of school governance, addressing such questions as whether parents were entitled to serve on governing boards, and if so, under what restrictions? Applications to charter authorizers often required the inclusion of a specific number of parent signatures and a statement as to how charter schools would involve parents in the school, as through parent compacts.[44]

Another emphasis in state charter laws was the goal of increasing school accountability, appearing in 84 percent of the laws. Charter schools as defined are performance-based schools that operate under a contract explicating a list of performance goals to be achieved by the end of the contract period. The idea was for authorizers to close down charter schools that persistently performed poorly and to renew the charter of those that performed better. School accountability also related to the pressure of choice and competition within a free market of public schools; if parents were empowered to choose a school for their child, then schools would compete with one another for students. Thus, charter schools that were not successful in attracting families—those not in demand by consumers—would be forced to close.

Most state legislatures also intended charter schools to have spillover effects to school districts, by increasing the capacity of the public education system and improving the performance of all district schools through increased competition between charter and non-charter public schools. Legislative goals grouped under the broad heading of "public school competition" (see figure I.2) include improving the achievement of all students, increasing competition, and increasing the capacity of the public school system. Interestingly, while increasing the capacity of school districts logically would produce more competition among schools in the marketplace, only two states—Florida and Illinois—were explicit about the goal of increasing competition among public schools, as in Florida's law that states the goal to "provide rigorous competition within the public school district to stimulate continual improvement in all public schools."[45] This result may reflect the political opinion among the electorate that competition in the public sector is unsavory. In contrast to framing it as competition, three states included as a purpose the goal to "improve the achievement of all students," and Tennessee, a more recent adopter with its charter law established in 2002, focused its preamble specifically on closing the achievement gap. A number of other states (e.g., California, Colorado, Florida, Illinois, Kansas, New Mexico, New York, North Carolina, Rhode Island) stressed improving achievement for targeted student groups, as in the Rhode Island law that mentioned a goal of serving "educationally disadvantaged" students; the Colorado law that specified targeting students who "because of physical, emotional, socioeconomic, or cultural factors, [are] less likely to succeed in a conventional educational environment"; the Kansas law that identified the purpose of reaching "pupils in special areas of emphasis in accord with themes established for charter schools"; and laws in California and New York targeting "academically low-achieving" students.[46]

As a summary of this section, Table I.1 presents a state-by-state overview of legislative intent as expressed in the various charter school laws.

OVERVIEW OF THE CHAPTERS

The purpose of this book is to explore the performance of charter schools across the array of goals set forth in state charter laws. Chapters 1 through 8 fall under three major domains, based on the empirical research on charter schools undertaken through a comprehensive review of relevant publications (see the appendix for our Notes on Research).[47] Each of the three domains—classroom, school/community, and system—includes chapters that present relevant findings. For instance, the classroom domain includes chapters that assess new roles for teachers, innovations in academic programs, and student performance outcomes.

To guide our discussion of findings within each domain, we offer a framework built around the goals of charter schools (see figure I.3). This framework serves as a guide for identifying the key inputs, interactions, and outcomes that underlie the charter school theory of action.

Starting with charter school classrooms—teachers, the academic program, and students—we work our way out to the school community and then to charter effects on the broader public school system, presenting findings relevant to each level in turn. The Reflections and Commentary chapter and the following Conclusion offer an opportunity to reflect on the past and look toward the future.

The remaining discussion in this Introduction gives a brief overview of how the main body of the book is organized.

Inside Charter Classrooms

We begin with a set of three chapters focused on the core of schooling—the teachers, the academic program, and the students. In chapter 1 we profile who is teaching in charter schools and how teachers

TABLE I.1

State-by-state comparison of goals behind charter school laws

	Teacher opportunities	Innovations in education programs	Student performance	School autonomy	Parent involvement	School accountability	Public school competition
Arizona (1994)						X	X
Arkansas (1995)	X	X	X			X	X
California (1992)	X	X	X			X	X
Colorado (1993)	X	X	X		X	X	X
Delaware (1995)		X				X	X
Florida (1996)	X	X	X	X	X	X	X
Georgia (1994)							X
Idaho (1999)	X	X				X	X
Illinois (1996)		X	X		X	X	X
Indiana (2001)	X	X			X	X	X
Iowa (2002)	X	X		X		X	X
Kansas (1994)	X	X	X	X		X	X
Louisiana (1997)	X	X		X		X	X
Maryland (2003)		X					X
Massachusetts (1993)		X				X	X
Minnesota (1991)	X	X		X		X	X
Nevada (1997)	X					X	X
New Hampshire (1995)	X	X			X		X
New Jersey (1995)	X	X				X	X
New Mexico (1993)	X	X	X	X	X	X	X
New York (1998)	X	X	X				X
North Carolina (1996)	X	X	X			X	X
Oklahoma (1999)	X	X		X		X	X
Oregon (1999)	X	X	X		X	X	X
Pennsylvania (1997)	X	X		X		X	X
Rhode Island (1995)		X	X	X	X	X	X
South Carolina (1996)	X	X		X		X	X

(continued)

TABLE I.1 *(continued)*

State-by-state comparison of goals behind charter school laws

	Teacher opportunities	Innovations in education programs	Student performance	School autonomy	Parent involvement	School accountability	Public school competition
Tennessee (2002)	X	X	X	X	X	X	X
Texas (1995)	X	X				X	X
Utah (1998)	X	X		X	X	X	X
Virginia (1998)	X	X				X	X
Wyoming (1995)	X	X		X			X
States per Goal	25	29	11	14	10	27	32
Percent Total*	78%	91%	34%	44%	31%	84%	100%

*10 laws do not have explicitly defined goals: Alaska (1995), Connecticut (1997), DC (1996), Hawaii (1999), Maine (2011), Michigan (1993), Mississippi (1997), Missouri (1998), Ohio (1997), and Wisconsin (1993).

Source:data compiled by reviewing O'Neill and Ziebarth, *Charter School Law Deskbook,* 2008–2009 Edition (Charlottesville, VA: LexisNexis, 2009).

are involved in school operations with respect to school governance. We consider the extent to which teachers have more professional opportunities through increased authority over the school's education program, its budget, and its staff. Are charter school teachers taking on new and different roles and responsibilities?

In chapter 2 we investigate the education programs charter schools use and the extent to which they are similar to and different from non-charter public schools. Are charter schools more likely to experiment with innovations in pedagogy and curriculum? What role does technology play in the education program? To what extent are individualized educational programs used, or innovations in delivery such as co-teaching models? What role do partnerships with outside organizations play in expanding education program offerings?

FIGURE I.3

Theory of action framework for charter school implementation

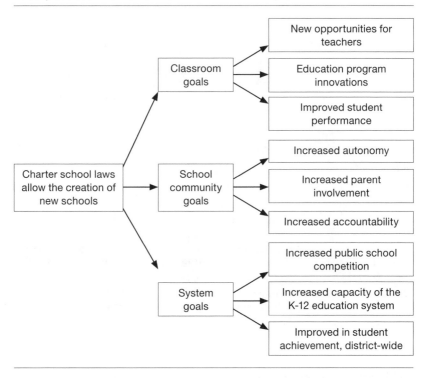

Chapter 3 reviews and synthesizes the vast amount of research on student performance in charter schools. The chapter opens with a review of the types of students who are attending charters and why they decided to attend. We then synthesize the array of studies examining student achievement in charter schools, many of which ask the question of whether students in charters outperform students in other public schools. In addition to student improvement, we consider charter performance on measures related to student engagement—attendance rates, disciplinary infractions, and turnover rates of students in charter schools.

The Charter School Community

The next three chapters consider the school community. In chapter 4 we examine how autonomy has shaped the charter school community. With expanded autonomy over the budget, school staffing, and the educational program, how has that authority been used and with what effects? Have school leaders used autonomy to experiment with innovative models of school leadership such as teacher leaders and co-principal arrangements? Has school-site autonomy led to greater financial efficiencies or other positive results? Are there conflicting policies at the state and local levels that have constrained school-site autonomy?

Chapter 5 investigates new roles for parents. Given the fact that charters are schools of choice, reformers envisioned more "authentic" opportunities for parent involvement. Many charter schools, some of which are founded by parents, stress the importance of parent involvement to student achievement. What are the tools and strategies charter schools are using to involve parents in their children's education, both at home and at school?

Chapter 6 delves into the area of accountability. In this chapter we take a look at how the exchange of more autonomy for more accountability has worked in practice. After a short rise of charter school closures due to poor performance, a recent study by the National Association of Charter School Authorizers concluded that many of their members were not doing what the job required—closing down poorly performing schools.[48] In this chapter, we explore what is known about authorizing practices—their evolution, their accomplishments, and their challenges.

The Education System

We then consider the impact of charter schools on improving the public education system as a whole. Charter schools were intended to serve as incubators of reform with the idea that the competition created by such schools would "spill over" into the broader public education system. Has increased competition among all public schools increased the capacity of the public education system? Have charter schools improved school performance and achievement levels for students as a whole? These questions are discussed in chapter 7.

The final group of findings, discussed in chapter 8, presents what is known about the unintended consequences of charter schools. The intended purposes behind the adoption of charter school laws are well known, but, as noted above, a burgeoning group of studies has highlighted the unintended or unplanned consequences—both negative and positive—that have emerged alongside the results that policy makers originally envisioned. One such consequence is the purported skimming of the best and brightest students by charter schools. A related question is whether charter schools have resulted in a (re)segregation of students along racial and ethnic lines. A further unintended consequence is the rise of charter management organizations, which were not imagined by the early policy champions of charter schools.

REFLECTIONS ON CHARTER SCHOOLS AND CHARTER SCHOOLING

As noted earlier, this book ends by offering an opportunity to reflect on what we know about charter school performance and what we still do not. Having spent the last few years taking a deep dive into the research on charter schools, we are not necessarily convinced that charter schools are the panacea for what ails public schooling. Nevertheless, we are fairly certain that charter schools are a reform that is here to stay.

In chapter 9, we invite five influential thinkers, including both charter enthusiasts and charter skeptics, to join the conversation, adding their own personal reflections on charter schools in particular and public schooling more generally. The commentators include Jeffrey Henig (Teachers College, Columbia University), Paul Hill (Center on Reinventing Public Education, University of Washington), Bruno Manno (Walton Family Foundation), Deborah McGriff (NewSchools Venture Fund), and Charles Payne (University of Chicago). The conversation explores crosscutting themes to examine the accomplishments and challenges associated with charter schools and the charter school movement. To help frame the conversation, we pose the following questions:

- In what ways, if any, have charter schools challenged the definition and boundaries of public education?
- Across the levels of the system—classroom, school, district— where have charters succeeded? Where have they fallen short?
- How is the relationship between charter and non-charter public schools changing? How is the role of charters in the education sector as a whole evolving?
- Most policies last ten to twenty years before being eclipsed by "the next big thing." What does the charter sector have to do in the next five years to assure its future?

We hope readers will also consider these questions as they peruse the chapters that follow. We conclude the book with a look at the future directions of the charter school movement. We also consider what will be the new avenues to explore, in view of the past twenty years of research on charter schools.

CHAPTER ONE

———■■■———

What New Opportunities Have Charter Schools Provided to Teachers?

IN 1988, ALBERT SHANKER, president of the American Federation of Teachers, introduced charter schools to the nation. In his weekly *New York Times* column, Shanker anticipated that charter schools would be created by groups of teachers (or parents with teachers) who wanted to develop new curricula or teaching strategies to improve student learning. It is not surprising, therefore, that nearly 80 percent of charter school laws include providing teachers with more professional opportunities as one purpose behind the adoption of the law (see the Introduction).

In our analysis of charter school laws, we included provisions that sought to create entirely new roles—such as teacher ownership of education programs and schools (which appeared in four state laws)—as well as those intended to expand roles for teachers (which appeared in twenty-five state laws), as in school governance and decision making. For example, the Florida law includes the goal of creating "new professional opportunities for teachers, including ownership of the learning program at the school site."[1]

Before we turn to an examination of the research around professional opportunities for charter school teachers, it is important to know who the teachers in charter schools actually are so that we know whether these "new opportunities"—to the extent that they exist—are being provided to a subset of teachers who transfer to charter schools from other public schools or to teachers drawn from a different pool, such as private schools, newly certified teachers, or fields outside of education.

A longitudinal survey of 160 elementary school teacher applicants from teacher preparation programs in six colleges in the Detroit area found that 45.6 percent reported submitting applications to teach at one or more charter schools.[2] Interestingly, these teachers exhibited statistically significant differences from the teachers who did not apply to teach at a charter school. The charter applicants were 9 times more likely to have also applied to teach at a private school, 5 times more likely to express a desire to teach in an urban setting, and 2.6 times more likely to live in a town with at least one charter school, suggesting a degree of familiarity with charter schools as public schools.

Knowing that the teaching force is segmented between charter and non-charter public schools—at least for elementary school teachers entering the field in Detroit—leads to the next question: are the two groups demographically different? An early study by Koppich, Holmes, and Plecki found that charter school teachers were demographically similar to non-charter school teachers, but more recent studies found some notable differences. First, charter school teachers tend to be younger. A comparison of teachers in Boston found that 68 percent of the staff in charter schools were under the age of thirty-two, while less than half of the staff in other public schools were in this age bracket; moreover, less than 10 percent of staff in charter schools were over the age of forty-nine, compared to 41 percent in other public schools.[3]

Other studies have found that charter school teachers attended more selective undergraduate institutions and earned higher SAT scores, although their GPAs were lower.[4] Unpacking these findings reveals the importance of the policy context: a study that examined teacher data from the 1999 Schools and Staffing Survey (SASS) found a link between the percentage of charter school teachers from competitive colleges and the certification requirements stipulated in state laws, a difference that was muted in subsequent years by the certification requirements of the federal No Child Left Behind Act. The finding that charter school teachers have lower GPAs than teachers from other public schools may well be related to the finding that charter school teachers also attended more selective undergraduate institutions. That is, charter school teachers might have lower GPAs because their college courses were more rigorous and challenging.

Brown, Wohlstetter, and Liu found that charter schools in California employed fewer credentialed teachers, many of whom had less teaching experience, compared to other public schools.[5] More than a quarter (28.2 percent) of the charter schools had a high percentage of teachers on emergency, interim, or waiver credentials compared to only 2.4 percent of non-charter schools. However, there is some evidence emerging that this trend is changing, perhaps in response to No Child Left Behind's mandate regarding teacher qualifications, as noted earlier. In California, the percentage of charter schools scoring in the bottom quartile of schools with a high number of underqualified teachers (those in their first or second year of teaching and teachers on emergency, interim, or waiver credentials) has dropped steadily over the years, from 34.5 percent in the 2004–2005 school year to 20.1 percent in 2008–2009.[6] Other studies of charter schools found that charter school teachers tended to work longer hours, with less job security and lower salaries, than teachers in other public schools.[7] These working conditions could explain why charter school teachers tend to be younger and less experienced than non-charter school teachers: the working conditions in charter schools may be more acceptable to them than to more veteran teachers. Indeed, Malloy and Wohlstetter reported that teachers from forty charter elementary schools in Los Angeles reported generally positive experiences working in charter schools, in spite of the less than favorable conditions.[8]

Hand in hand with working conditions, teacher mobility has been shown to be greater in charter than in non-charter schools.[9] Drilling down into the types of teachers who tend to leave charter schools, one study found that charter school teachers who leave their positions generally have lower GPAs and lower pass rates on credentialing exams than those who stay.[10] Another study found that years of experience and years at their current school were the strongest predictors of teacher attrition from among a range of teacher qualification variables.[11] Variance in turnover rates was also attributed to "involuntary attrition"—the freedom granted to charter school leaders to hire and fire teachers—as well as to the particular type of charter school, with conversion charters experiencing lower teacher turnover than start-ups.[12] An analysis of the 1999–2000 SASS data found that higher teacher attrition in charter schools was predominantly attributed to the preponderance of charter schools located in urban areas. While 30 percent of teachers at urban charters leave their teaching positions after the first year, only 17 percent in rural charter schools and 18 percent in suburban settings do so.[13] However, another study found that charter schools in Wisconsin had lower teacher attrition in urban areas than did non-charter public schools.[14]

With these characteristics of charter school teachers in mind, we now turn to the question of whether charter schools fulfill the legislative goal of providing new opportunities for teachers. As noted earlier, we categorized provisions in state charter laws concerning teacher roles into two groups. The first set offers teachers entirely new professional opportunities; the second set seeks to expand the opportunities that many public school teachers already have. We examine each of these in turn.

DO CHARTER SCHOOLS PROVIDE COMPLETELY NEW OPPORTUNITIES FOR CHARTER SCHOOL TEACHERS?

In order to look at whether charter schools provide new opportunities for their teachers, it is a useful exercise to describe what we envision as the "typical" non-charter public school teacher's position in a school. Historically, teachers were given a fair bit of control over what went on behind the (often closed) door of their classroom. Referred to by Lipsky as "street-level bureaucrats," public school teachers are the subset of government employees who implement the education policies mandated by the state and federal government.[15] As such, there is a dichotomy between those delivering instruction (teachers) and those setting policy decisions, generally the district or state. The increased emphasis on state test scores in the past two decades has reduced teachers' control of their classroom in many cases, as districts and states tie funding to the school's adoption of a specific curriculum package. Most notable, perhaps, is the adoption by some districts (including Los Angeles) of a "scripted" curriculum for English language arts. This lack of professional discretion contrasts with the goal of charter schools to provide new opportunities for teachers.

With this picture of teaching in mind, there are two main areas in the research that examine ways in which states have empowered charter school founders to think outside the box when it comes to their teachers: school "ownership" and alternative pay structures.

Do Charter Schools Provide Teachers New Opportunities through School "Ownership"?

Across the country, there are a handful of teacher-operated charter schools, in which groups of teachers hold the charter. They typically operate as a "professional practice" or as a formal worker cooperative. In the 2006–2007 school year, for example, twenty-eight charter schools in eight states were affiliated with EdVisions, a cooperative established in Minnesota in 1992 with a mission to "create and sustain small, project-based, teacher-led, democratic schools."[16] These teacher-run schools minimize the traditional dichotomy between management and labor by creating an arrangement that allows teachers to continue teaching while assuming administrative roles. In more traditional arrangements, teachers must give up classroom duties if they want to move up in the field of education.

Not all teachers want to move up existing hierarchical tiers, yet many do want to expand their roles. For example, in a national sample of teachers in 2003, Public Agenda explored teachers' attitudes for new arrangements in its research for *Stand By Me: What Teachers Really Think About Unions, Merit Pay and Other Professional Matters*. It found that 58 percent of teachers were somewhat or very interested "in working in a (charter) school run and managed by teachers"; this included 65 percent of under-five-year teachers and 50 percent of veteran (20 years and over) teachers.

However, despite the apparent attractiveness of the idea, teacher-run schools make up a small minority of charter schools. Education|Evolving (E|E), a St. Paul–based "policy design shop" that has championed the teacher professional partnership idea nationwide, notes that the principal obstacle to implementing teacher-run schools is the common assumption that teachers must be employees. Reform initiatives designed to improve teaching and learning generally take place within an employer/employee framework. An additional challenge is teachers' lack of experience working collegially to run a business. Most do not conceive of this possibility when they begin teaching and were not trained as education majors to run a business. Thus the vast majority of charter schools do not provide teachers with the new professional opportunity of school ownership.

Do Charter Schools Provide Teachers Alternative Pay Structures?

As noted in chapter 4 on autonomy, three-quarters of state charter school laws allow some (for example, newly created) or all of the charter schools in their state to operate outside of the district collective bargaining agreement. This has resulted in experimentation with alternative pay structures, such as a merit pay system.[17] In their analysis of the 1999–2000 SASS data, DeArmond, Gross, and Goldhaber found that about one-third of charter schools use merit incentives.[18] A study of personnel practices in six states—Arizona, California, Hawaii, North Carolina, Rhode Island, and Texas—found that 43 percent of charter schools offered merit pay compared with 13 percent of districts. However, the study's authors found that the school's performance had a greater influence than the merit pay system on both the quality and quantity of applicants to the school.[19]

Although more common than teacher ownership, the idea of merit pay is foreign to many teachers. A longitudinal review of one school's design, implementation, and evaluation of its merit pay system found that one important feature of the system was that "the impetus for change came primarily from staff, making it more of a bottom-up change than often is the case when compensation or evaluation systems are changed."[20] The system was phased in, starting with new teachers who had less familiarity with the traditional salary structure than more veteran teachers; the authors write that "by phasing-in the new pay system, the school also hoped that veteran teachers would gain trust in the new system as well as confidence that the new system could be a positive change force."[21]

DO CHARTER SCHOOLS PROVIDE EXPANDED OPPORTUNITIES FOR CHARTER SCHOOL TEACHERS?

The next question is whether charter schools offer expanded opportunities for teachers. One such area for teachers to experience new roles might be in decision-making rights, which we will discuss in chapter 4 on charter school autonomy. Another area might be around the opportunity for teachers to engage in deeper collaboration with their colleagues. While communities of practice (e.g., professional learning communities, vertical teams) certainly exist in non-charter public schools, might charter schools be implementing such professional opportunities for teacher growth as the rule rather than the exception? In a similar vein, might charter schools provide teachers more opportunities to use data to inform instruction? These two questions are examined below.

Do Charter Schools Provide Expanded Opportunities for Teacher Collaboration?

The research to date is spotty, with little conclusive evidence of widespread practices that promote increased opportunities for teacher collaboration. One limitation of the research in this area is that it tends to report on isolated case studies. For example, one study of a charter school serving predominantly special education students examined the collaboration among parents, teachers, administrators, and community members to meet the needs of its students, while another looked at teacher collaboration in an elementary school that partnered with a university to improve math instruction.[22] Yet another study profiled a sole charter school teacher and found that the stress of working in a charter school with limited resources and high expectations was balanced by the collaborative environment of mentorship.[23] While these single case studies do show evidence of high levels of teacher collaboration in the charter schools they examine, they are by no means generalizable to the broader charter school population.

While single-case-study research clearly limits the ability to make broad generalizations about teacher roles in charter schools, studies that do include larger sample sizes produce a multifaceted picture that likewise prevents sweeping generalizations. As in other research areas, the national research on teachers highlights the variation found in different school contexts. For example, an analysis of the 1999–2000 SASS data compared teacher community at charter and non-charter elementary schools, finding that charters generally have stronger teacher community, though the difference is small and varies along a number of dimensions including authorizer type, collective bargaining status, and principal control of staffing policies.[24] Teachers' opportunities for collaboration also varied in different management arrangements. In a qualitative study of six charter schools operated by three EMOs, the level of professional community in the charter school depended on several factors, including the role of the EMO in designing structures that facilitated substantive teacher interaction, the presence of strong leaders who shared the company's mission but operated independently and were committed to building and supporting professional community, and the ability to design or support strong programs for collective and individual professional learning.[25]

Do Charter Schools Provide Expanded Opportunities for Data Use?

Another area where we might potentially see new opportunities for teachers is in data use. Data use—also referred to as data-driven decision making—has become common in the non-charter public system, but there are several reasons to hypothesize that data use might be more prevalent in charters than in other public schools. For one thing, charter school leaders have more decision rights than most non-charter schools. Not only can they reschedule the school day to create time to examine data, but they also have more control to put in place remedies such as site-based professional development tailored to the particular needs of teachers, reassignment of students to interventions, and quick adoption of a new instructional program. Furthermore, the pressure of accountability—in theory, charters can be closed for poor performance—creates a catalyst for improving school performance before the end of the charter period. However, as in collaboration with colleagues, the current research on data use in charter schools tends to be limited to small-scale rather than national studies.[26] For example, in case studies of data-driven decision making in two charter schools, Petersen found that teachers at one charter school were taught how to work with data as part of a weeklong "teacher academy," and test scores from the prior year were used to plan for the coming year.[27] While Zimmer and Buddin found that California charter schools across all grade levels placed a greater emphasis on mentoring and coaching than the typical non-charter school, the research on data use in non-charter schools also finds cases where such practices are increasingly robust.[28]

QUESTIONS FOR THE FUTURE

What we observed in the literature was that many charter schools that are new and emerging are trying to "build the plane while flying it" and do not have time to develop policies that are not directly related to recruiting teachers and families, and to the core of schooling—teaching and learning.[29] While a handful of charter schools have created entirely new professional opportunities through teacher ownership of the school, and more are experimenting with merit pay, the research does not provide a clear case that charter school laws have expanded the opportunities that many public school teachers already have.

The finding that over half of the newly credentialed teachers in one area did not consider applying to charter schools could indicate one of two things: knowledge about what charter schools are is still limited, or charter schools are not offering teachers a more enticing alternative to working in a non-charter school. Adapting policies to identify, recruit, and retain teachers is going to be increasingly challenging as the charter school sector continues to grow. We know from earlier studies of school-based management that while teachers were given significant decision-making authority, they were rarely trained in the rudiments of how to develop a school budget and how to conduct effective committee meetings—creating an agenda, holding committee members to the agenda, and engaging members in next steps before the meeting adjourns. Charter school teachers need similar training if they are going to be given these roles.

There are three clear areas of unanswered questions around teachers' roles in charter schools: 1) charters' hiring practices, 2) the effects of incentive-based reward programs, and 3) factors contributing to lower teacher qualification rates in charters. In terms of hiring practices, it is unknown how these practices differ across different types of charter schools and across different contexts. Also unknown is whether charter schools' hiring practices affect strategies for recruiting, hiring, and retaining teachers in the broader education system. For example, if charter schools in an area are found to attract teachers from more prestigious universities, does the school district offer a signing bonus in response? There are also unanswered questions about merit pay programs and their potential organizational and financial effects for school districts with increasingly smaller budgets.[30] Finally, little is known about the factors—including turnover rates, a school's professional community, teacher demographics, and resources invested in developing quality teachers, among others—that may help explain the differences between charter and other public school teachers.[31]

———■·■———

CHAPTER TWO

What Education Program Innovations Have Charter Schools Used?

A KEY DRIVER OF THE CHARTER MOVEMENT was the desire to free up public schools from constraints that were thought to impede their ability to design innovative education programs. Charter school proponents stressed the need for deregulating schools—pushing for waivers from state and local regulations—and for shifting decision-making responsibilities closer to school communities. These principles of deregulation and decentralization, at least in theory, would allow the education programs to be tailored explicitly to the needs of a particular student population.

At the same time, the idea of charter schools was built on the power of markets. Charter schools, as schools of choice, would seek to fill or create a niche in the schooling market that was not readily available to other public school students. It followed, given the strong push for market accountability (see chapter 6), that charter schools that failed to attract students to their brand of education would ultimately be forced to close for lack of "customers." This line of thinking, bolstered by a small group of states, pioneered the idea that successful charter schools were to be laboratories for innovation. More than 90 percent of state charter laws included as one of the purposes behind the law to encourage school communities to use their autonomy in the classroom to experiment, innovate, and create new educational options for students.

At the start of the movement in the early 1990s, Joe Nathan of the Center for School Change at the University of Minnesota, together with Alex Medler, a policy analyst at Education Commission of the States, conducted a national survey of states with charter school laws. One of the earliest of such studies, it asked respondents to describe how their legislatures envisioned education in charter schools and how it might differ from what was currently offered in public schools. A number of the respondents noted that their state laws directly mentioned that charter schools were intended to prepare students for the twenty-first century. Legislatures were also interested in having charters serve at-risk students and dropouts, including nontraditional students over the age of eighteen. The use of technology and personalization were stressed in charter laws as well, suggesting that instructional methods might differ from those used in existing public schools.[1] For instance, charter schools associated with the Edison Company management organization provided each family with a laptop, while Fenton Avenue Charter School, one of the first charters in California, introduced the idea of a virtual classroom into their school by ensuring that every fifth grader had a computer on his or her desk.

Not surprisingly, a sizable body of research on charter schools has tried to assess the extent to which innovation has actually occurred. In this chapter, we review some of the education program innovations in charter schools to illuminate the ways in which charter founders have used their decentralized decision-making authority to reconsider what schools should teach and how students should be taught. At the same time, we recognize that observers, including some of the original champions of charter schools, have been disappointed that the basic anatomy of schools has been tinkered with but not really reinvented. We discuss this debate later in the chapter.

A TOUR OF INNOVATION IN CHARTER SCHOOLS

Rather than inventing completely new ways to educate students, charter schools seem to have adapted to fit niches in the public school market in which non-charter public schools have not been especially successful, either by design or as a consequence of enrollment. Some charter schools have been developed to serve students identified as "failing" or "at-risk," or to better meet the needs of racially or culturally diverse students.[2] As such, instructional programs have been redesigned to meet those students' needs, focusing on college preparation, team teaching, immersion and bilingual education, or a "back-to-basics" design, among others. Finally, the schools themselves have changed, adopting cyber or hybrid models and revitalizing schools as community centers through partnerships with local neighborhood groups.

Designing Education Programs to Meet Students' Needs

Charter schools seem to have adapted to fit niches in the school market in which typical public schools have not been especially successful. In their surveys of over seven hundred charter and matched non-charter elementary, middle, and high school principals in California, Zimmer and Buddin found that the idea of targeting a specific subset of students was more common in charter than non-charter schools.[3] Similarly, Ausbrooks, Barrett, and Daniel's examination of the organizational characteristics of 159 charter schools in Texas found that mission statements in nearly half of the schools focused on students who had already dropped out of school or who were at risk of doing so.[4] Authors hypothesized that these findings may be due to charter laws: many states have allowed charter schools to draw students from outside of traditional attendance zones, freeing charter schools to target specific types of students.[5] Another factor may be related to charters as schools of choice that must compete with other schools for families and students. While early critics of charter schools feared the schools would target white middle-class students, research has found that charter schools actually served disproportionate numbers of low-income and minority students.[6]

Many public schools, particularly in urban areas, have not been particularly effective in educating at-risk students. Not surprisingly, one of the first charter schools to open in Minnesota targeted at-risk students and dropouts up to the age of twenty-one. City Academy High School, located in St. Paul, uses individual learning plans, community service projects, and an alternative schooling model that includes a year-round school schedule with the aim of retaining and graduating students at risk of dropping out.[7] Since then, other charters have opened that have focused on new uses of technology (such as online courses for credit recovery or blended curricula) along with other alternative pathways to graduation. Providing alternative options at the high school level, in particular, may be part of an effective strategy to reduce high school dropout rates and encourage college matriculation.[8] While the population of charter schools started out with the majority at the elementary school level, the trend has been changing slowly as charter schools age and expand to serve higher grades.

In addition to focusing on at-risk students, some charter schools take it a step further, encouraging not just high school completion but also college attendance. Consider Lionel Wilson College Preparatory Academy, located in a historically low performing district in northern California. It aims to graduate all of its students into colleges and universities. The school develops a college-going culture by "introducing college as a natural continuation of each student's academic career, providing a college preparatory curriculum and any academic support needed for student success, guiding students through the college preparation and application processes, and presenting students and families with options for overcoming financial barriers to higher education."[9] From 2004 to 2006, the school exceeded the state graduation rate target, and every one of its graduates was accepted to at least one four-year college or university.

Looking at small urban high schools (those enrolling fewer than seven hundred students), Gross and Pochop found that 66 percent of charter schools versus 48 percent of non-charter schools reported offering at least one college-focused program.[10] In a four-year longitudinal case study of a college-preparation high school, scholars found that the flexibility of the charter structure allowed counselors to foster college counseling and student social supports in new ways.[11]

Beyond attending to at-risk students and college preparation, in a study that included sixteen charter high schools nationwide, Yatsko, Gross, and Christensen found that half set out to serve a specific group of students such as African American, Spanish-speaking Hispanic, or Native American populations, while three more had adjusted their programs to better serve a distinct group of students in their surrounding district.[12] These foci included a mission that addressed how the school's programs should focus on students' specific academic needs, cultural background, and special interests. A host of descriptive studies identified schools that had missions focused on a culturally and linguistically relevant curriculum, such as bilingual education; an academic program targeting Muslim youth; and other cultural studies programs.[13] Similarly, Quach presented a case study of New Hope Charter School, a school that focused on special education services for children ages sixteen to twenty-one who had severe physical and developmental challenges.[14]

In their content analysis of thirty-eight charter school applications in ten cities in California, North Carolina, and Texas, Christensen and Rainey found that charter schools approached the design of the education program by selecting from a "menu of possibilities" based on the needs of the students they serve.[15] The menu included five core components of the school: target population, curriculum, instructional approach, classroom structure, and student services. In this way, the authors argued, charter schools were not developing new education programs so much as packaging existing programs and processes in new ways. For example, thirty of the thirty-eight charter schools studied used a student-centered instructional approach, such as project-based, constructivist, or experiential learning; thirty-one utilized multi-age or multigrade classrooms, "looped" classes with teachers over multiple school years, used block scheduling, or organized teachers into teams that worked with the same group of students; and fourteen had alternative grade configurations such as K–8, 6–12, or K–12.[16] A given school often used more than one of these approaches, thus combining "modular" elements in often unusual ways.

Another study—Gross and Pochop's mixed methods study that included analysis of the 2003–2004 Schools and Staffing Survey (SASS) as well as a review of charter school applications in three states—found that on average, charter schools had smaller class sizes and longer school years, spent more time on instruction, and customized programs for struggling students.[17] In her examination of student rewards and other incentive programs in 186 charter schools in seventeen states, Raymond found that among the 57 percent that reported developing and using a student reward system, 93 percent of these covered both academic effort and behavior; such reward programs were found to have a positive impact on student achievement gains in reading, but not in math.[18] A study of charter schools in New York City identified the following school design and educational practices as positively associated with charter school academic success:

- The length of time that a school has been open
- A longer school day/year than traditional school calendars
- A greater number of minutes devoted to English during each school day
- A small-rewards/small-penalties disciplinary policy
- Teacher pay based somewhat on performance or duties, as opposed to a traditional pay scale based strictly on seniority and credentials
- A mission statement that emphasizes academic performance, as opposed to other goals

In this study, the authors also note that class size, optional after-school programs, and math and reading curriculum were found to have no significant effect on academic success, except for the Open Court Reading program and the Everyday Mathematics curriculum, which have significant negative impacts.[19]

In a survey of more than two hundred principals in both charter and non-charter schools in Michigan, Mintrom found that charter schools were 17 percent more likely to offer innovative curricula than their counterparts and 8 percent more likely to use innovative instructional techniques.[20] Based on their analysis of the 2003–2004 SASS, Christensen and Lake concluded that charter schools "seem to be fulfilling some of their early promise for innovation around instruction, teacher hiring, and professional practice."[21]

New Role for Technology

With the push to prepare students for the twenty-first century, charters in the early years of the movement experimented with technology.[22] Neumann's ethnographic study of High Tech High noted the way the school had infused technology into its curriculum: the use of technology "is not an end but rather a means, a tool for investigation that contributes to the effective conduct of student projects."[23] High Tech High and similar schools with a technology focus use project-based learning in which students work in teams, while other schools built on the special education approach and stress personalization.

In addition to individual charter schools that have incorporated technology into their core approach to education, virtual or cyber charter schools have become more prevalent within the population of charter schools. Variously known as virtual, non-classroom-based, distance, online, or home charter schools, these models differ "from conventional schools by relying on parents and the Internet to deliver much of their curriculum and instruction while minimizing the use of personnel and physical facilities."[24] Few laws explicitly have defined or regulated cyber charters, causing difficulties in determining per-pupil funding, establishing accountability measures, defining enrollment boundaries, and monitoring the wave of traditional homeschoolers who are entering public education.[25]

Parents, teachers, and students gave a variety of reasons when explaining their choice of a cyber school, including: the flexibility of curriculum, pacing, and scheduling; a lack of confidence in the public schools in terms of teaching, learning, and safety; and the fact that the program is free, compared with homeschooling or private school.[26] Hipsky and Adams' qualitative study of a cyber charter school in Pennsylvania found that the online setting provided intense focus for students who were prone to social distractions in "bricks and mortar" settings.[27] Students reported enjoying the two-way dialogue between the student and instructor, receiving immediate response and private feedback through discussion boards and e-mails. Drawbacks to the cyber model included the difficulty in providing specialty classes, like gym or music, and the lack of peer-group interaction and interpersonal relationships.[28]

The research on virtual charter effectiveness has focused more on policy and management-related issues than on student outcomes.[29] Only a small number of case studies of cyber charter schools has been conducted; outcomes are varied when these schools were compared with classroom-based programs. For example, Klein and Poplin's study of six California Virtual Academies found that the schools scored above the state averages in fifteen of eighteen grade categories in English. Math performance was weaker, however, with only two of eighteen schools on a par with state averages.[30] Shoaf's mixed-methods study of the effectiveness of a virtual charter school in Ohio found that the students at the cyber charter school performed lower than the state average based on all public schools, but the cyber school performed better when compared to a similar non-charter public school.[31] On the other hand, Zimmer, Gill, Booker, Lavertu, Sass, and Witte found that students had substantially lower achievement gains while attending virtual charter schools than they experienced in non-charter schools.[32]

Partnerships with Community Organizations

Unlike non-charter public schools, which depend on district central offices for resources such as funding, personnel, facilities, administrative support, and curriculum and instruction, charter schools must identify their own sources for these essential goods and services. The need to amass resources on their own poses a significant challenge for charter schools, especially newly established, stand-alone schools.[33]

Since charter schools cannot look "up" to school districts for assistance and support, they often have to look "out" to other organizations for the essential resources they need to survive and thrive. These operational challenges create incentives for charter schools to form partnerships with outside organizations. Typically described as a win-win situation, a partnership is defined as organizations working together to solve issues of mutual concern based on the benefits of collective action, addressing needs and problems that are beyond the capacity of either organization to resolve alone.[34]

Exemptions from many district and state regulations enable charter schools to seek partnerships more readily than other public schools, and laws in many states encourage such outside involvement. Well-constructed partnerships can provide a host of needed resources such as facilities, funding, and administrative support, as well as less tangible benefits, such as increased visibility, governance expertise, and help in getting charter school applications approved. In some cases, the organizations provide or supplement the curriculum that forms the focus of the school. In still other cases, partnerships with social services providers offer wrap-around resources that help meet the needs of the school's students and their families.

At the same time, partnerships with charter schools can help the partner organizations achieve their own goals. Often, partner organizations are able to expand the services they provide by partnering with a charter school. For example, museums generally have education outreach functions in addition to their core mission, and partnering with a charter school provides a means to integrate the museum's programs into a school's curriculum rather than being limited to the peripheral curricular supplements provided to non-charter school students in a once-a-year field trip. Lacina, Hagan, and Griffith's case study of a charter school in eastern Texas described how a partnership between the charter school and a university aided the school's personalization of a workshop approach to teaching and evaluating student writing.[35]

A small handful of studies have examined the involvement of outside organizations. One such study found that partnerships have provided a host of financial, political, and organizational resources to charter schools.[36] Table 2.1 provides examples of the common resources different types of partners provide.

State laws have been found to influence the development of partnerships between charter schools and other organizations in a variety of ways, including charter application requirements, the charter approval process, or the eligibility of partners.[37] Reviews of the charter school legislation in each state found that state laws often facilitate the formation of certain partnerships—most often, those with community organizations—while restricting others, generally with faith-based or for-profit organizations.[38] Despite these restrictions, interviews with leaders from state department of education charter school offices and state charter school resource centers reported that partnerships between charter schools and other organizations were fairly prevalent and wide-ranging in terms of the organizations involved, including nonprofit, for-profit, and public sector organizations, as shown in table 2.2.[39]

TABLE 2.1

Resources that partnerships provide

Type of Partner	Examples of Resources
Community-Based	• Name recognition to attract students • Legitimacy to aid in charter school application approval • Board expertise
For-Profit	• Grants, donations, and loans • Credibility to secure financing • Back-office support
Faith-Based	• Facilities • Fundraising expertise

TABLE 2.2

Types of organizations that have partnered with charter schools

Economic sector involvement	Types of organizations
Nonprofit sector	Community-based organizations (CBOs)
	Cultural institutions
	Educational institutions
	Faith-based organizations
	Nonprofit charter management organizations (CMOs)
	Private foundations
	Race/ethnic-based organizations
	Social services providers
	Advocacy organizations
For-profit sector	Education management organizations (EMOs)
	Local businesses
Public sector	Cultural institutions
	Educational institutions
	Public-health providers
	Government (city offices, mayor's offices)
	Police departments

Source: Adapted from Wohlstetter et al., "Improving service delivery in education through collaboration," *Social Science Quarterly* 85, no. 5 (2004): 1086; and from Smith, Wohlstetter, and Hentschke, *A Guide for State Policymakers: Partnerships Between Charter Schools and Other Organizations* (Washington, DC: National Resource Center on Charter School Finance and Governance, 2008): 5.

HOW INNOVATIVE ARE THE PROGRAMS CHARTER SCHOOLS OFFER?

Despite the reports by some scholars that innovation occurs within the charter space, Lubienski provided a frank discussion around what we define and understand to be "innovation."[40] He used three dimensions to understand the idea of innovation: At what level within the institution does the practice represent change (e.g., classroom versus administrative)? To what extent is the practice established and familiar or original and unique? And to what extent does the practice appear at the local, state, or national levels? Using fifty-six reports of innovation in charter schools, Lubienski found that "although some organizational innovations are evident, classroom strategies tend toward the familiar."[41] Organizational, administrative, and structural changes were prominent, such as experimenting with parent contracts, merit pay for teachers, and smaller class size. While Lubienski did take note of some innovative classroom-level practices (e.g., the use of technology as a way to support or provide instruction; individualized instruction), on the whole, charter "innovations"—practices such as hands-on learning, cooperative learning, or a "back-to-basics" approach— were all strategies that could occur (and have occurred) within the traditional district setting. He argued that if the role of charter schooling is to provide "laboratories for R&D" for new instructional practices, they are not, in fact, meeting this goal. Similarly, in a study of the local education markets in two Midwestern cities, Lubienski found that charter school messages were similar to private schools. The author concluded that "rather than diversifying options, the marketing seems to emphasize a rather monolithic model of schooling built around characteristics commonly associated with more established private schools."[42]

Others also claim that classroom innovation in charter schools is limited.[43] Ausbrooks et al., in their review of promotional information from Texas charter schools, claim that while the school administrators may be "thinking about innovative school environments, at least in the design of the school . . . [and though] one of the cornerstones of charter school legislation was the freedom for schools to be innovative in teaching methods, yet 20 percent of the schools list no unique teaching method."[44] Similarly, in their study of charter high schools, Yatsko, Gross, and Christensen argued, "Even among the highest performers, few charter schools have deviated much from the traditional American notion of high schooling."[45] Finally, in their interviews with two charter school policy experts in each state, Smith, Wohlstetter, and Brewer found that charter schools have produced some notable innovations in teacher empowerment, community partnerships, and governing board operations.[46] However, the authors concluded, "despite these pockets of innovation, the movement as a whole employs fairly traditional . . . models."[47]

QUESTIONS FOR THE FUTURE

On the whole, charter schools' education programs point to limited innovation in curriculum and instruction. Education program differences between charter and non-charter schools have been noted, but there has been little evidence of charter schools developing completely new education programs. Innovation typically has emerged in how instruction is delivered; for instance, many charter schools, both site-based and cyber, and most recently blended or hybrid charter schools, have increased the use of technology.

The demands of state and local accountability policies may drive curriculum and pedagogy to be more traditional or test-focused.[48] To increase innovation within the sector, some suggest that increased state investment in incentives for creative educational designs, as well as authorizers that encourage innovative proposals, can help improve the diversity of the charter sector.[49] One author suggests that the charter sector has matured to the point where charters' roles as "labs of innovation" can be leveraged, with best practices shared with the larger public school community.[50] Finally, we wonder if the discussion has shifted away from innovation (for innovation's sake) and more toward replicating what works according to evidence.

Research on educational programs used in charter schools is very limited, in part because of the difficulty in researching successful charter school "islands" across states. This is an important constraint for researchers and for practitioners looking to spread new knowledge within the charter movement and to non-charter schools. Within states, there has also been limited investigation of education programs used in charter schools. The online Promising Practices Compendium Highlighting Innovations in Charter Schools (sponsored by the University of Southern California) profiles educational programs—bilingual education, project-based learning, special education and

STEM programs, to name a few—in California charter schools, but across the United States few if any other compendia have emerged, perhaps because of the difficulty in discovering and defining the term "promising practice," as well as the lack of funding to support this aspect of charter school research.[51]

In more recent research on education programs in charter schools, three primary topics for future investigation have been proposed.[52] First, are charter schools engaging in educational programs that differ from other neighborhood public schools? And if so, to what extent are charter schools importing educational programs versus developing their own? Second, in implementing their educational programs, do charter schools encounter any challenges, as in identifying a program that fits with student needs or acquiring money for professional and program development within the school context? Finally, which educational programs are successful at improving student achievement, and can similar approaches be useful beyond the charter sector?

CHAPTER THREE

——— ■■■ ———

Have Charter Schools Increased Student Performance?

THE GOAL OF INCREASING student achievement in charter schools is a key component of charter school accountability, serving as a primary consideration in decisions by authorizers to renew or revoke school charters (see chapter 6 on accountability for more information about charter authorizing). This is not too surprising considering the increased emphasis on student achievement at the federal level in the No Child Left Behind Act, which requires schools to disaggregate student achievement data by subgroups—racial/ethnic, special education, free and reduced-price meals, and limited-English proficient—to aid reformers in monitoring school progress in closing the achievement gap. Likewise, the Obama administration's Race to the Top initiative requires that state accountability systems include student-level data information systems to facilitate tracking individual student progress over time.

We include under this broad legislative goal of improving student achievement those state laws that specifically mention closing the "achievement gap" (as in Tennessee's law that includes a goal to "improve learning for all students and close the achievement gap between high and low students"). We also include charter laws stating that a key purpose of charter schools is to improve student learning and achievement for targeted students, a provision specified in nine states' charter school laws (as in the New York law that includes a goal of increasing student achievement "with special emphasis on expanded learning experiences for students who are at risk of academic failure.")[1]

In this chapter, we consider the evidence about charters and improved student achievement. The chapter also tackles the question of what charter school student performance is compared to—charters to charters, or charters to non-charter public schools? While most of the research examines the outcome measures of student achievement, we also observed that more attention is being paid in recent years to leading performance indicators. For example, schools that have reduced instances of student discipline problems (leading indicator) likely may have students who achieve at higher levels (outcome measure) than schools that do not, so we consider studies of leading indicators as well as research that measures student outcomes. We first delve into the empirical findings about charters and student achievement and then move on to explain some of the contextual factors.

WHAT IS KNOWN ABOUT STUDENT ACHIEVEMENT IN CHARTER SCHOOLS?

There has been considerable experimentation with approaches to studying student achievement in charters, and over time the methods have become far more sophisticated and rigorous. The kind of data used to examine student achievement outcomes has matured from data that look at student achievement at a single point in time, to longitudinal data, then to virtual matched pairs of students, and finally to the "gold standard" of evaluation—random assignment of students to schools through the charter school lottery process. In table 3.1, we offer comparisons of findings from a variety of studies designed to answer the question of whether charter schools have achieved the goal of increasing student achievement.

TABLE 3.1

Summary of findings from studies of charter school achievement

	STUDY SAMPLE		
Data source	**Multiple schools/cities in one state**	**All charter schools in a single state**	**Multiple states and cities**
Single point in time cross-sectional results	Okpala, Bell & Tuprah (2006)—Average results positive in reading and math		
Longitudinal school-level results	Barr, Sadovnik & Visconti (2006)—Average results insignificant in reading and math		Miron, Coryn & Mackety (2007)—Average results negative in reading and math
Longitudinally linked student-level data	Booker, Gill, Zimmer & Sass (2009)—Average results positive for reading and math; Center for Research on Education Outcomes (2010)—Average results positive for reading and math; Lavertu & Witte (2009)—Average results insignificant in reading, positive in math; McDonald, Ross, Bol & McSparrin-Gallagher (2007)—Average results positive for reading and math; Witte, Weimer, Shober & Schlomer (2007)—Average results positive for reading and math; Zimmer & Buddin (2006)—Average results insignificant in one location and negative in one location; Zimmer, Blanc, Gill & Christman (2008)—Average results insignificant	Bifulco & Ladd (2005)—Average results negative in reading and math; Bifulco & Ladd (2006)—Average results negative in reading and math; Bifulco & Ladd (2007)—Average results negative in reading and math; Buddin & Zimmer (2005)—Average results positive in elementary reading and negative in elementary math and high school math and reading	Zimmer, Gill, Booker, Lavertu, Sass & Witte (2009)—Average results insignificant in five out of seven locations and negative in two locations

(continued)

TABLE 3.1 *(continued)*

Summary of findings from studies of charter school achievement

	STUDY SAMPLE		
Data source	**Multiple schools/cities in one state**	**All charter schools in a single state**	**Multiple states and cities**
Virtual matched pairs			Center for Research on Education Outcomes (2009)—Average results negative in reading and math
Random sample of students "lotteried-in" to charter schools	Hoxby & Rockoff (2005)—Average results positive in reading and math; Hoxby & Murarka (2008)—Average results positive in reading and math; Hoxby, Murarka & Kang (2009)—Average results positive in reading and math		

In looking at table 3.1, it is difficult to identify trends or generalizations across studies. Given the variety of methods and samples, it is not surprising that findings continue to be mixed. In their October 2011 meta-analysis, Betts and Tang report that there is "compelling evidence that charters under-perform traditional public schools in some locations, grades, and subjects, and outperform traditional public schools in other locations, grades, and subjects."[2] Location was seen to matter in the widely publicized 2009 report by the Center for Research on Education Outcomes (CREDO), which found that only 17 percent of charter school students outperformed their non-charter counterparts in math. The report, which included student-level data from sixteen jurisdictions (a mix of single cities and whole states) aggregated at the school, state, and national levels, found that charter school performance varied widely by location, with the variation "over and above existing differences among states in their academic results."[3] Gains in growth ranging from 0.02 to 0.07 standard deviations were found in five locations: Arkansas, Chicago, Denver, Louisiana, and Missouri. Lower average charter school student growth ranging from −0.01 to −0.06 standard deviations was found in six locations (Arizona, Florida, Minnesota, New Mexico, Ohio, and Texas), and four locations (California, the District of Columbia, Georgia, and North Carolina) had mixed results or no significant differences between charter and other public schools. Prior to the CREDO report's release, Hoxby and Murarka concluded that student achievement in New York City charter schools tended to surpass achievement in non-charter schools.[4] The primary author of the CREDO report subsequently reanalyzed her data for charter schools only in New York City and agreed with Hoxby's findings: achievement of students in New York City charters outpaced those of students in other public schools.

One potential explanation for the mixed findings is that charter schools serve some students less well than others. Several studies found that student outcomes differed depending on students' race or ethnicity.[5] However, the directions of these differences—positive or negative—varied by study. For example, CREDO's 2010 longitudinal study of six years of data (the 2003–2004 through 2008–2009 school years) found that in New York City, African American and Hispanic students enrolled in charter schools did significantly better in reading and math compared to their counterparts in non-charter public schools.[6] However, their earlier longitudinal analysis of over 1.7 million records from more than 2,400 charter schools in fifteen states and the District of Columbia found that minority populations had lower learning gains in charter schools compared with "virtual twins" in other public schools.[7] King found that the percentage of minority students in Arizona charter schools had a negative and statistically significant relationship with outcomes, as did Wolfram who reported that African American and Hispanic students in EMO-managed charter schools in Michigan had lower student outcomes.[8]

There were also mixed findings as to how charter schools fare based on students' socioeconomic status. Using the nationally representative 2003 National Assessment of Educational Progress (NAEP) data, Lubienski and Lubienski found that student demographics were more important than school sector in predicting academic achievement, finding "far more variation within schools than between them."[9] In three case studies of economically distinct charter schools, Bancroft found strong links between socioeconomic status and student outcomes.[10] Although all three schools faced financial difficulties, the school with wealthier parents was able to supplement the school's budget with their own donations. Teachers at the low-income schools, on the other hand, faced a difficult time providing services to help students "catch up." Similarly, Okpala, Bell, and Tuprah's study of forty-eight middle schools in a North Carolina school district, half charter and half non-charter, found that positive student outcomes in the charter schools were related to higher family incomes.[11] In their study of 357 middle schools in Colorado, Chamberlin similarly found that poverty was by far the biggest predictor of student outcomes in charter schools, as is the case more generally in public education.[12] These studies, however, do not address the question of whether these students are better off in charters as opposed to non-charter schools.

CREDO's more recent study makes that contribution, finding that low-income charter school students outperformed their non-charter school counterparts.[13]

In addition to results differing based on socioeconomic status, the CREDO study also found that English language learners realized significantly better learning gains in charter schools, while special education students fared no better in charter schools than did their counterparts who remained in non-charter public schools. However, Downing, Spencer, and Cavallaro's qualitative case study of a new-start charter elementary school concluded that high numbers of special education students had a negative effect on overall school performance—again, a common conclusion in the research on student achievement in public schools.[14]

Research has also pointed to the variation in student outcomes based on grade levels served. As in other areas, results have been mixed, especially at the high school level. Zimmer and Buddin's 2006 study of charter school performance in Los Angeles and San Diego found that in Los Angeles, charter high school students scored 1.1 percentile points lower in reading and 1.3 percentile points higher in math than comparable non-charter students.[15] In San Diego, by way of contrast, the pattern is reversed by subject areas—reading scores in charter high schools were 1.5 percentile points higher in charter high schools while math scores were 1.7 percentile points lower. The CREDO study found that charter school students in elementary and middle school grades have significantly better results than their peers in non-charter schools, but students in charter high schools and charter multilevel schools have significantly worse results. Edwards, Barondess, and Crane, on the other hand, found that charter high schools in California scored modestly higher on the Academic Performance Index (API), a summary measure.[16] Interestingly, the Booker, Gill, Zimmer, and Sass study of charter schools in Chicago found positive outcomes only in the charter high schools that also included middle school grades.[17]

Not only do grade levels make a difference in results, but so too does the subject tested, according to some studies. Betts and Tang's review of fourteen prior studies found positive results in some grades and subjects over others. Charter schools in these studies outperformed non-charter schools on reading tests in elementary schools and on math tests in middle schools. Conversely, charter schools often significantly underperformed in high school reading and math.[18] In their longitudinal study of student outcomes in Philadelphia, however, Zimmer, Blanc, Gill, and Christman found a small positive effect for charter high schools and a small negative effect for charter elementary schools in both math and reading.[19] In contrast, Zimmer, Gill, Booker, Lavertu, Sass, and Witte's analysis of longitudinally linked student-level data from eight jurisdictions—Chicago, Denver, Milwaukee, Philadelphia, San Diego, and the states of Ohio, Texas, and (for one analysis) Florida—found no evidence that charter school performance varied systematically by grade level.[20]

While the "mixed results" conclusions may be the truest statement about student achievement two decades into the movement, there also may be other explanations relating to the charter context that, in turn, lead to difficulties in identifying an appropriate sample of charter and non-charter schools. We discuss some of the specific challenges to assessing charter school performance in the following section.

WHY CAN'T THE EVIDENCE ON CHARTER SCHOOLS OFFER A GENERAL CONCLUSION ABOUT PERFORMANCE?

In a review of the first decade of charter school research, Bulkley and Fisler identified a range of challenges to evaluating achievement in charter schools:

- *Variations in charter laws across states:* numbers and types of authorizers; some states allow for only new-starts (no conversions)
- *Variations in the population of charter schools:* age of the school; school design (e.g., on-site, virtual, hybrid schools), and education program

• *Methodological issues:* aggregated versus disaggregated performance data; student versus school-level data, sample size[21]

In the section that follows, we delve into these issues by examining results from studies that investigate variations in charter laws and the charter population, and the extent to which these variations appear to influence student outcomes. We also examine the impact of methodological issues on studies of charter school performance.

Variations in Charter Laws Across States

What does the research say about the effects of charter authorizers? There is some evidence that authorizer type—school district, university, or state body—affects student outcomes, as does the matter of whether a charter applicant has a choice of authorizers to submit its application to. For example, CREDO found that states with multiple authorizers had less successful charter schools as judged by student achievement results.[22] Specifically, "states that empower multiple entities to act as charter school authorizers realize significantly lower growth in academic learning in their students, on the order of −0.08 standard deviations. While more research is needed into the causal mechanism, it appears that charter school operators are able to identify and choose the more permissive entity to provide them oversight."[23] Similarly, Zimmer, Gill, Booker, Lavertu, Sass, and Witte suggest that the great variation in charter performance in Ohio could potentially be related to the fact that the state's charter law allows an unusually diverse group of organizations to serve as charter authorizers, although this hypothesis has not been empirically tested.[24]

What does the research say about the performance of new-start charters and existing schools that have converted to charter status? In considering charter laws across the United States, 88 percent of states allow both conversions and new-start charter schools. However, five states (Michigan, Mississippi, Nevada, New Mexico, and South Dakota) allow only new-starts. Over the decades, studies have investigated whether new-starts or conversions have a steadier track record in producing higher student achievement. The preponderance of evidence suggests that new-start charter schools have better track records, but there are a few studies that conclude the opposite.

Zimmer, Blanc, Gill, and Christman found that new schools (compared to existing schools that converted to charter status) scored better in math and reading.[25] Attending a new-start charter school also has been linked to improvement in student discipline. Imberman reported a drop of 0.6 to 0.8 disciplinary infractions per year in new-start charter schools compared to conversion charter schools and non-charter public schools.[26]

In the Zimmer et al. study of eight locations mentioned above,[27] the authors concluded that conversion charters had significantly greater effects on high school graduation than new-start charter schools. The study confirmed earlier research by Imberman that had a far smaller sample. Imberman's quantitative study of an anonymous large urban school district found that conversion charter schools had a slightly higher passing rate on state tests than non-charter schools and new-start charter schools.[28]

Variations in the Population of Charter Schools

What does the research say about the effects of the age of the school on student achievement? In addition to the common finding that student performance dips during the student's first year at a charter school, the age of the school appears to matter as well.[29] In an analysis of test scores in North Carolina from five cohorts of students in third grade, Bifulco and Ladd found that low performance in the early years of a school was not uncommon.[30] The authors hypothesized that "one potential explanation for these findings is that many of North Carolina's charter schools were in their first years of operation and thus were grappling with the challenges of starting a new school."[31] Rerunning their analysis, the authors found that "the negative effects of attending a charter school are considerably greater for students in newly opened schools than for students in charter schools that are more established."[32] In their more recent eight-state study, Zimmer et al. concluded that charter schools in most locations had difficulty raising student achievement in their first years of operation, typically producing achievement results that fell short of those of local public schools.[33] This was consistent with prior research and may not be a charter-specific phenomenon; opening a new school is challenging, regardless of whether or not the school is chartered.

Similar effects have been found in studies of charter school networks. In a study in Michigan of charter schools affiliated with National Heritage Academy, Wolfram concluded that the number of years a school in the network had been in existence was positive and statistically significant in all twelve regressions.[34] Its strongest effect was in eighth grade, adding 2.88 points to science scores, 3.2 points to social studies, and 6.3 points to math scores annually.

We found only one study with a mixed message. Zimmer, Blanc, Gill, and Christman concluded that there was "no significant differences in impacts between those schools that have been in operation for three years or less and for charter schools that have been in operation for four or more years," leading the authors to conclude that the age of the school was not a strong influence on student achievement.[35] However, they offered a caveat: attending a charter school in its first year has a small but statistically significant negative effect on students in math.[36] There is not much disagreement among the empirical studies about the negative achievement pattern known as "first-year effect."[37] Steps to mitigate the effect might include charter founders working more closely with authorizers during the start-up period; accessing additional start-up grants from funding authorized under the Federal Charter Schools Program and the Walton Family Foundation Public Charter Startup Grant program; and replicating or growing successful models.[38]

What does the research say about the effects of charter school design on student achievement?   Charter schools are created by their founders for a variety of reasons. Some have missions focused on the environment, the arts, or science and technology (for more academic program innovations, see chapter 2). In addition to the founders' personal visions, some states encourage charter schools to serve at-risk populations, while others require charter schools to serve student populations that are representative of the surrounding district. Lawton's review of prior research noted that the complexity of different charter school missions made performance generalizations impossible.[39] Not only do their missions differ, but charter school also have varying designs, with some being newly created from scratch and others converted to charter status from existing public schools; some are classroom-based "bricks and mortar" schools while others operate as virtual schools. With these differences in mind, several studies have attempted to investigate whether some school missions and designs are better than others in raising student achievement. For example, Buddin and Zimmer's quantitative study looked at student achievement in four types of charter schools in California: charter schools that convert from non-charter status, charter schools that start from scratch, charter schools that rely primarily on classroom-based instruction, and charter schools that have a significant portion of instruction outside the classroom.[40] The authors found that new schools compared to conversion schools scored better in math and reading. In contrast, Imberman's quantitative study of an anonymous large urban school district found that conversion charter schools had a slightly higher passing rate on state tests than non-charter schools and new-start charter schools.[41]

Methodological Challenges in Charter School Studies

What constitutes a good comparison group?   One of the toughest challenges in identifying a reasonable comparison group, composed of all charters or non-charter public schools, is the idiosyncratic way charter schools evolve. New-start charters, which now represent the majority of charter schools in the United States, tend to launch with a grade or two the first year and then add grades as the school ages. With a new charter elementary school that has grades K–1, what is a comparable comparison group? There clearly are no regular public schools that would be a good match; finding a comparable charter school is also challenging. This predicament is further complicated by the fact that some charter schools choose to have atypical grade configurations—kindergarten through twelfth grade, or a charter school that combines middle school and high school, serving students in sixth or seventh grade through twelfth grade. Again, the incidence of comparison schools among the charter and non-charter sectors is extremely low.

Interestingly, the problem of finding an appropriate comparison group across state and district jurisdictions has led to some innovative research methods. Consider the case of the methods used by CREDO in 2009. Lead author Margaret Raymond developed and applied the idea of virtual matched pairs in which each charter school student is matched with a virtual twin based on the student's demographics, English language proficiency, and participation in special education or subsidized lunch programs.

Also notable is the fact that student-level data are not routinely released to the public. While this may ultimately change in the few states that received Race to the Top grants and are required to create student-level information systems, Miron, Evergreen, and Urschel in a 2008 study highlighted the extent of the problem: aggregated data were used in nearly half of the forty-seven studies they reviewed.[42] This is problematic in that the use of aggregated student outcomes produced different findings than when disaggregated data were presented.[43]

Researchers have also highlighted the importance of tracking individual students over time.[44] When individual students were tracked over time, debate ensued about the efficacy of the two most common approaches: panel data that track student performance before and after entering a charter school, and randomized pairs of students who did and did not win entrance into a charter school. In the former approach, Hoxby and Rockoff argued that the students who switched from a non-charter school to a charter school "are too atypical for the results to be interpreted in a straightforward way . . . [The studies] rely entirely on an unusual group of students who switch from regular public schools to charter schools late in their elementary-school careers."[45] Furthermore, this group of longitudinal studies ignored the population of charter school students who entered a charter school in the early years (kindergarten through as late as second grade), since prior test scores were not available for these students.

On the other hand, Betts and Tang argued that the primary weakness of lottery-based studies was that they only included schools for which the number of applicants exceeded the number of available seats; as noted above, schools with lotteries, these authors argued, were likely to be higher performing than charter schools without over-subscribed lotteries.[46]

Different methodological considerations aside, Miron et al.'s review of forty-seven charter school studies concluded that advances in the sophistication of study methods have not changed the overall conclusion of mixed results. Among the studies using more sophisticated methods, the authors found that nineteen had positive findings, twelve had mixed findings, and sixteen had negative findings.[47]

Leading Indicators: Student Persistence and Student Discipline

While outcome measures have been the focus of many empirical studies, studies over the past decade have explored the effects of leading indicators—that is, indicators that generally occur in advance of improvements in student achievement, adding in its prediction. Leading indicators of interest focus on student persistence in school and student discipline, based on the notion that if the first is high and the second is low student achievement will likely improve.

Not surprisingly, the longer students remain in a charter school, the better they perform.[48] As mentioned earlier in this chapter in our discussion of new-start charter schools, students tend to lose ground academically in their first year at a charter school.[49] CREDO's study, for instance, found that "first year charter students on average experience a decline in learning, which may reflect a combination of mobility effects and the experience of a charter school in its early years. Second and third years in charter schools see a significant reversal to positive gains."[50] In a study of student outcomes among third graders in North Carolina, Bifulco and Ladd found that students "usually make small gains during their first year in a charter. This is true regardless of how long the school has been operating . . . [In contrast,] students who choose to remain in charter schools do not continue to make smaller gains than students in traditional public schools after their initial year in a charter school."[51] Wolfram estimated the precise benefit of time spent at National Heritage Academy, a network of charter schools in Michigan, and concluded that the strongest, statistically significant effect was in seventh grade reading, where each day at the charter school added .012 points to a student's test score, or 4.38 points per year.[52]

The one exception to the general conclusion that student gains accumulate the longer a student stays at the charter school is a 2009 study by Lavertu and Witte examining gain scores on math and reading tests in Milwaukee: "The positive impact of charter schools on achievement (relative to traditional public schools) declines as the number of years a student has attended a charter school increases."[53] This finding suggests that more information is needed—is Milwaukee's charter school environment different in some way from other states or school districts?

Just as it makes intuitive sense that test scores increase with a student's duration in a particular school, high student turnover rates can be expected to cause test scores to dip. A few studies have suggested that a student's arrival at a charter school and student mobility are confounded. In one study that looked at charter schools in Philadelphia, the authors found that student mobility was highest during the student's first year of attendance.[54]

The relationship between student persistence in school to student success has led to some of the strongest and most extreme statements. Bifulco and Ladd's study, mentioned above, concluded, "High rates of student turnover may account for as much as one-third of the negative impact charter schools have on student performance."[55] Lavertu and Witte's conclusions went a step further, asserting that "instability in school attendance in urban school districts . . . proves to be the most significant determinant of student achievement in all of our statistical models."[56]

High attrition rates also appear to artificially inflate a school's test results, if low performing students exit a school. Henig's review of seven studies of student achievement in the Knowledge is Power Program network (KIPP) found that attrition in KIPP schools is "high and seemingly selective."[57] Low performing students left KIPP more often than higher performing students, although Henig concluded that "the evidence does not go so far as to suggest that attrition fully accounts for the observed KIPP advantage."[58]

A number of empirical studies have also used additional indicators of student success. From the beginning of the charter movement a frequent mission of many charter high schools was to prepare students to be college and career ready, with principals often being held accountable for the percentage of students who graduated from their schools and went on to four-year colleges. Consider the case of the Preuss School in San Diego, which was recently named the top charter school in the state of California based on its academic and financial performance, and also was ranked number eight in the *U.S. News and World Report*'s list of the best charter high schools in the nation.[59] The latest graduation class (2012) had every graduating senior accepted to four-year colleges.[60] Charter high schools are still experimenting with the best way to track success on these indicators. In 2009, the Bill and Melinda Gates Foundation launched the College-Ready Promise, which funded four Los Angeles charter management organizations to identify and promote effective teaching practices so that more students graduate college-ready.

From several empirical studies in Florida, which has a management information system that can track students in public schools from kindergarten through to college, a positive and statistically significant relationship was found between attending a charter school and graduating from high school and enrolling in college.[61] Other similar studies conducted in Chicago found that charter school students had an advantage of approximately 7–15 percentage points in the probability of graduating from high school and an advantage of 8–11 percentage points in the probability of enrolling in college.[62]

QUESTIONS FOR THE FUTURE

The wide variations in findings around student outcomes in charter schools suggest that further refinements are needed in the use of student- and school-level data. Questions remain as to whether results are based on student characteristics or on the effect of the charter school itself.[63] There also have been calls for using mixed-method, multiple-measure approaches to evaluating student outcomes.[64] For instance, districts, states, and authorizers can not only look for patterns in the achievement of individual student gains (e.g., growth models), but can also consider trends in enrollment over time, turnover rates, dropout rates, discipline, safety, attendance, wait lists, parent/teacher/student satisfaction, and college acceptance and persistence rates.[65] There are also unanswered questions around different outcomes based on different governance models.[66]

It seems reasonable to assume that assessment of charter school effects will only get more complex as the research gets more granular, as in studies of charter schools with varying levels of autonomy and studies that look at the success of charter schools serving particular student populations. Future studies will likely be able to get into the "black box" of charter schooling to unravel the effectiveness of different instructional approaches on student achievement, such as project-based learning, bilingual education, team teaching, and theme-based approaches. Looking ahead, it is also likely that with the Obama administration's focus on accountability and incentives to create student-level data systems, there will be far more states and districts with the capacity to track individual student progress across all public schools (as in Florida), which ultimately will help solve some problems relating to comparison groups and also the disaggregation issue.

■ ■ ■

CHAPTER FOUR

How Have School Leaders Responded to Greater Levels of Autonomy?

AUTONOMY FROM RULES AND REGULATIONS is central to the charter school concept. The theory of action argues that if school leaders are given autonomy and the level of accountability is also increased, then charters, as schools of choice, will use their freedom in creative ways to design programs that attract parents and students. Increased autonomy over school decisions, it is posited, will also enhance local buy-in and commitment among school staff, parents, and communities. Further, the local educators (rather than district, state, or federal administrators) who are closest to students and have the most knowledge about students' educational needs are expected to have more decision-making power in three key areas: curriculum, budget, and staffing. Better decisions in these areas—how and what students should be taught, how the money is spent, and who should be hired and fired—ideally will lead to more effective instruction in the classroom and ultimately to improved student achievement. Across the United States, fourteen charter laws cite increased school-level autonomy as a key driver behind the legislation.

In recent research, scholars have explored not only the extent to which charter schools are, in practice, autonomous organizations, but also how charter school leaders use their enhanced autonomy to operate in better, different, or more innovative ways. In this chapter, we first review findings on the variation in autonomy across charters in the United States. Next, we explore the ways in which schools and school leaders have used their autonomy, considering who is involved in decision making and what kinds of decisions—budget, staffing, curriculum—they are making. Finally, we discuss limitations to school-level autonomy and challenges as perceived by local stakeholders.

VARIATION IN AUTONOMY ACROSS STATES AND WITHIN SCHOOLS

Providing additional autonomy to individual schools has been an aspect of numerous reforms over the past forty years, including those aimed at alternative schools, magnet schools, and schools using site-based management, in addition to charter schools. In general, autonomy encompasses the ability of individual schools to make budgeting, staffing, and educational decisions that drive both internal governance/operations and external relationships. The strength of this autonomy derives in part from the extent to which the school is independent from higher levels of government and in part from the ability of stakeholders to make changes and decisions for the school. In some cases, charter legislation grants charters blanket waivers, while in other cases, schools are required to apply for waivers individually. Research has shown that considerable variation exists in the level of autonomy charter schools experience, depending on state laws, collective bargaining status, the school's relationship with its authorizer, and the presence of partnerships with management organizations and faith-based organizations, among others.[1]

In What Areas Is Autonomy Being Exercised?

Education programs Individual examples of different education programs surfaced in the review of research undertaken for this book. Margolis's ethnographic study describes a sixth- to twelfth-grade charter school that runs eleven months a year in which students receive quarterly narratives outlining their progress instead of traditional grades.[2] Whole-class instruction and large-group activities have been replaced with individualized learning; interdisciplinary projects are presented to a panel instead of evaluating learning through standardized tests. Learning outside of the traditional classroom is emphasized, with students engaging in job shadowing, internships, and self-directed field trips.

WestEd, for the U.S. Department of Education, profiled charter schools that had used their autonomy to develop curricular programs that helped close the achievement gap for students.[3] Gateway High School in San Francisco, for instance, is a school designed to offer an individualized college preparatory curriculum to a wide range of learners; the school aims to have at least 25 percent of its student body be students with a diagnosed disability. The Toledo School for the Arts in Toledo, Ohio, fully integrates an arts-based curriculum—with investments in music, dance, theater, and visual arts—into a rigorous academic program that meets state standards.[4]

In more comprehensive studies we also see patterns where charters use their autonomy to create targeted instructional programs to groups of students. In a study of alternative paths to high school graduation using data from sixteen case studies in three states combined with national Schools and Staffing Survey (SASS) data, Yatsko, Gross, and Christensen found that the autonomy afforded to charter schools enabled them to provide a more highly focused mission and educational program, adapt instruction to meet the unique needs of the school's students, focus on college preparation, build community through small class and school size, and experiment with atypical grade and administrative configurations.[5] In a review of the existing studies, Mickelson, Bottia, and Southworth found that more than 80 percent of the charter schools in the research they reviewed had a theme or curricular focus such as math and science or the arts; students' academic needs (gifted and talented, special education); instructional approaches (Montessori, experiential learning); or ethnic themes.[6] Similarly, Ausbrooks et al. identified the top five teaching methods from Texas charter schools in 2000–2001, namely individualized, self-paced instruction (54 percent); parent and community involvement (34 percent); computer-assisted learning (34 percent); practical skills/school-to-work (28 percent); and an emphasis on fine arts/languages (22.6 percent).[7] (For greater depth on the types of curricular programs and administrative innovations that take place in charter schools, please see chapter 2.)

Budget   Autonomy granted to charter schools has produced different ways of educating students, sometimes for reduced costs. Grosskopf, Hayes, and Taylor compared student achievement gains with school inputs in urban charter and non-charter public schools in Texas and found that charter schools were substantially more efficient than non-charters.[8] The authors hypothesized that charter schools' efficiency was due to the freedom they enjoyed from many of the regulations governing the operation of other public schools, including a state-mandated maximum pupil-teacher ratio of 22 to 1 in grades K–3, a requirement to have counselors and a nurse once student enrollment reached a specified minimum, and a mandatory minimum salary scale.

Staffing   State charter school laws regulate whether teachers engage in collective bargaining separately from the local teacher union, as part of the local teacher union, or not at all.[9] Green Dot Public Schools is one charter network that has experimented with developing a union contract for its teachers as a way to attract and retain high-quality teachers. Under the union agreement, only a few centralized policies are included in the contract: salary, health care, class size, and number of workdays. For example, teachers are given explicit decision-making authority in setting school policy, including the school's budget, calendar, and curriculum, and there is no tenure, seniority preference, or probationary period for new teachers. The contract is thirty-three pages, compared with the three-hundred-plus-page contract governing most Los Angeles public schools.[10]

As for union involvement, state laws determine whether charter schools are subject to the local school district's collective bargaining agreement, often with provisions allowing for waivers and amendments to be negotiated between the charter school and the local school district. Table 4.1 shows the collective bargaining status of charter schools in each state. Lake's national, qualitative study found that when charter schools are involved in labor negotiations, these negotiations "are converging on two priorities: trying to preserve what they see as mission-critical labor expectations and the ability to build and sustain a high-quality team."[11]

Allowing teachers to be unrepresented or to bargain separately from the local teachers' unions may support new innovations in personnel practices, hiring and termination processes, induction programs, professional development, and evaluation/compensation systems.[12] Using the 1999–2000 SASS data, Cannata found

TABLE 4.1

Collective bargaining provisions in state charter school laws

	Charter schools are not part of the school district's collective bargaining agreement	Charter schools are part of the school district's collective bargaining agreement	Charter schools authorized by an LEA are part of the district's collective bargaining agreement	Charter schools can choose whether to remain part of the district's collective bargaining agreement	Charter schools can form their own collective bargaining unit	Conversion charter schools remain part of the district's collective bargaining agreement
Alaska		X				
Arizona	X					
California				X	X^e	
Colorado	X			X	X	
Connecticut				X	X	
Delaware					X	X
District of Columbia	X					

(continued)

TABLE 4.1 *(continued)*

Collective bargaining provisions in state charter school laws

	Charter schools are not part of the school district's collective bargaining agreement	Charter schools are part of the school district's collective bargaining agreement	Charter schools authorized by an LEA are part of the district's collective bargaining agreement	Charter schools can choose whether to remain part of the district's collective bargaining agreement	Charter schools can form their own collective bargaining unit	Conversion charter schools remain part of the district's collective bargaining agreement
Florida					X	
Georgia	X					
Hawaii		X				
Idaho					X	
Illinois						X
Indiana					Xf	X
Iowa		X				
Kansas		X				
Louisiana		X				
Maryland		X				
Massachusetts		Xa				
Michigan			X		Xg	
Minnesota				X	X	
Missouri	X					
Nevada					Xh	
New Hampshire					X	
New Jersey				Xc	Xf	X
New Mexico	X					
New York					Xi	X
North Carolina	X					
Ohio					X	X
Oklahoma					X	
Oregon				Xd	X	
Pennsylvania	X					
Puerto Rico	X					
Rhode Island		X				

(continued)

TABLE 4.1 *(continued)*

Collective bargaining provisions in state charter school laws

	Charter schools are not part of the school district's collective bargaining agreement	Charter schools are part of the school district's collective bargaining agreement	Charter schools authorized by an LEA are part of the district's collective bargaining agreement	Charter schools can choose whether to remain part of the district's collective bargaining agreement	Charter schools can form their own collective bargaining unit	Conversion charter schools remain part of the district's collective bargaining agreement
South Carolina				X[c]	X[f]	X
Tennessee					X	
Texas			X			
Utah	X					
Virginia		X				
Wisconsin		X[b]				
Wyoming	X					

Source: Adapted from Education Commission of the States, "Are Charter Schools Bound by School District Collective Bargaining Agreements?" (Denver: 2010).

a. In Massachusetts, Horace Mann charter schools are part of the school district's collective bargaining agreement, but Commonwealth charter schools are not.

b. In Wisconsin, "instrumentality" charter schools are part of the school district's collective bargaining agreement, but non-instrumentality charter schools are not.

c. In New Jersey and South Carolina, new-start charter schools can choose whether to remain part of the district's collective bargaining agreement.

d. In Oregon, charter schools authorized by an LEA have the choice to remain part of the school district's collective bargaining agreement.

e. ECS reports that in California, charter schools can choose whether to remain part of the district's collective bargaining agreement, form their own collective bargaining unit, or organize independently, in which case "it is generally subject to the state's education collective bargaining laws" (http://www.ecs.org/clearinghouse / CharterSch/California.pdf).

f. In Indiana, New Jersey, and South Carolina, new-start charter schools can form their own collective bargaining unit.

g. In Michigan, non-LEA authorized charter schools can form their own collective bargaining unit.

h. In Nevada, teachers on a leave of absence from their previous district-run school retain their collective bargaining coverage related to district employment status.

i. In New York, start-up charter schools that enroll more than 250 students are considered a separate bargaining unit of the district's employee organization until charter expansion or renewal.

that teachers in charter schools reported higher levels of teacher community than their counterparts in the other public schools; the author hypothesizes that charters' flexibility around staffing helped increase teacher camaraderie due to the lack of assignment by seniority and the ability to hire teachers that share the school vision.[13] However, Sam, Smith, and Wohlstetter caution that "teachers may be ill-equipped to make informed bargaining decisions because they lack experience performing this role."[14]

Beyond their potential ability to hire outside of a collective bargaining agreement, charter schools have also been able to target hiring of teachers with specific academic and interpersonal skills.[15] This hiring process can include matching new teachers with the individualized school mission and potentially bringing in school community members in the process, such as students, other teachers, family members, and local businesses. (For further information, see chapter 1 on teacher involvement.)

Who Is Vested with School Autonomy and How?

Teachers Related to the goal of increased autonomy was the idea that local decision makers, mainly teachers, would become more involved in making decisions related to schooling. This, in turn, would lead to greater teacher commitment to and ownership of the charter school. Researchers have examined this goal by assessing the extent to which charter school teachers felt they had more decision-making authority over the education program, staffing, and budgeting than their counterparts in non-charter public schools.

Some research found that decision making was more inclusive in charter schools than in non-charters.[16] The Malloy and Wohlstetter interviews with forty teachers in six urban charter elementary schools in California found that the teachers felt involved in school decision making when the principals created a "sense of team."[17] Such psychological beliefs translated into positive behaviors; teachers frequently served on grade-level teams and on vertical work teams to create particular schoolwide initiatives, such as redesigning the school report card or developing a school program to boost family engagement.

A case study of four charter schools in California—two new-starts and two conversions—found that teachers in the two new-start charter schools and in one of the conversion schools reported they experienced increased autonomy.[18] However, teachers from both conversion schools felt restricted by district oversight, especially regarding accountability measures. All of the teachers reported feeling constrained by state-level accountability measures.[19] Teachers from three out of the four charter schools felt that they had an adequate level of autonomy in the domain of curriculum, with teachers from only one school reporting feeling restricted by their affiliated charter management organization. The authors concluded that teacher input was expanded in the areas of instructional activities, curricular innovation, hiring and evaluation of faculty, and decision making concerning how the school budget should be spent.

In contrast, Crawford's surveys of nearly four hundred teachers from a mix of charter and non-charter schools in Colorado and Michigan found that teacher perceptions of autonomy in these two states were statistically indistinguishable between the two types of schools; in fact, teachers in non-charter schools "believed that they had more opportunities to participate in the decision-making process."[20] Through surveys with one hundred and forty teachers and administrators from four non-charter elementary schools, Marshall, Gibbs, and Greene, on the other hand, reported that non-charter teachers expressed a desire for more autonomy and believed that charter schools would allow teachers more independence than the non-charter setting.[21]

Some researchers have focused on the specific issue of teacher involvement in school governance as opposed to operational or management decisions related to the school's academic program, finances, and staffing. Sam, Smith, and Wohlstetter conducted a legislative review of forty-one state laws and interviewed eighty state leaders to explore how charter schools nationwide involve teachers in school governance.[22] The findings suggested that teachers are not formally included in school governance in most charter schools, with a few "pockets" of schools that involve their teachers in the decision-making process more than the rest. This finding of sporadic involvement was mirrored in the overwhelming majority of state laws that did not include specific provisions around teachers' roles in school governance (see table 4.2). While four state laws required teachers to be involved in founding roles such as development of the charter, and six states required a teacher to be part of a charter school's governing board (and two allow it but do not require it), thirty-one state charter school laws were silent on the issue. Mintrom noted that charter school governing boards in Michigan reported that they always consulted teachers when making policy decisions in 28 percent of charter school cases compared with 11 percent of the non-charter public schools.[23]

Similarly, through interviews and observations at a charter school serving sixth to twelfth grade, Margolis found that although teachers enjoyed the greater autonomy they experienced, some teachers felt like it was a greater burden.[24] These teachers hoped that administrative duties would be relegated to administrators and instructional duties to teachers. When having to balance both types of work, teachers expressed feeling overwhelmed, the result of which has been associated with faster teacher burnout.

School leaders Researchers have also considered if and how school leaders have responded to greater school-level autonomy. Given the theory that charter school autonomy supports more decision making at the school site, a number of past studies investigated the extent to which this decentralization had actually occurred.[25] A few studies examined whether charter school leaders have the autonomy to exercise their leadership skills—particularly by comparing charter school principals' perceptions of autonomy to their non-charter school counterparts.[26]

In one survey of California school leaders in 2000–2001, Zimmer and Buddin found that charter school principals reported having greater control over decision making than their counterparts in other public schools.[27] However, Adamowski, Therriault, and Cavanna, through their interviews and survey of thirty-three

TABLE 4.2

How states address the issue of teacher involvement

	Require teacher involvement in the development of the charter	Require teacher representatives on the governing board	Teachers eligible for governing board membership	Teachers not allowed to sit on governing board	Teachers participate in a separate grievance committee	Allow teachers to engage in their own collective bargaining	No relevant provisions
Alaska							X
Arizona						X	
Arkansas							X
California						X	
Colorado							
Connecticut		X				X	
Delaware	X	X				X	
District of Columbia	X		X				
Florida						X	
Georgia							X
Hawaii		X				X	
Idaho						X	
Illinois						X	
Indiana						X	
Iowa							X
Kansas							X
Louisiana				X			
Maryland						X	
Massachusetts						X	
Michigan							X
Minnesota		X				X	
Missouri				X			
Nevada		X				X	
New Hampshire			X			X	
New Jersey					X	X	

(continued)

TABLE 4.2 *(continued)*

How states address the issue of teacher involvement

	Require teacher involvement in the development of the charter	Require teacher representatives on the governing board	Teachers eligible for governing board membership	Teachers not allowed to sit on governing board	Teachers participate in a separate grievance committee	Allow teachers to engage in their own collective bargaining	No relevant provisions
New Mexico							X
New York						X	
North Carolina							X
Ohio						X	
Oklahoma						X	
Oregon						X	
Pennsylvania						X	
Puerto Rico							X
Rhode Island							X
South Carolina	X						
Tennessee						X	
Texas							X
Utah							X
Virginia		X					
Wisconsin	X						
Wyoming						X	

Source: Sam, Smith, and Wohlstetter, "Involving teachers in charter school governance" (Los Angeles: National Resource Center for Finance and Governance, 2008).

charter and non-charter school principals, identified an "autonomy gap"—a difference in the authority principals think they need in order to be effective and the authority they actually have.[28] While both groups experienced the autonomy gap, charter school leaders reported having greater autonomy across most key school functions, including staffing and personnel decisions, allocation of resources, and determining instructional time.[29]

A range of variables may affect the level of autonomy for charter school leaders. Through an analysis of the nationally representative Schools and Staffing Survey, Gawlik identified two institutional barriers—state and district policies—as significant to perceived principal autonomy. As noted earlier, the type of charter school—start-up versus conversion—may also affect principal autonomy; Gawlik found that start-up charter schools generally had more autonomy than non-charter schools, while conversion schools did not.[30] Principal autonomy was also linked to state laws concerning unionization and to whether principals had hiring and firing rights.[31] Charter school laws also had an impact on teachers' working conditions and hiring practices.[32]

The extended set of responsibilities that charter school leaders face may also play a role in how they are able to use their autonomy. In addition to the many challenges associated with school management and operations, charter school leaders encountered a variety of unique charter-specific responsibilities. A job analysis of the charter principal role by six charter school principals in one state indicated that a varied set of knowledge, skills, abilities, and other leadership attributes were required to be a successful charter school principal. These skill sets fell into eight categories: 1) curriculum and instruction, 2) personnel management, 3) student personnel, 4) building administration, 5) home-school-community relations, 6) school-system relations, 7) personal and professional development, and 8) other unscheduled activities.[33] Similarly, in a longitudinal case study of a converted charter school, Jacobson, Johnson, Ylimaki, and Giles found that principals' leadership facilitated the success of teacher professional development and the school overall.[34]

However, in three separate surveys of charter school principals, many charter school leaders reported struggling with the responsibilities of leading their school and taking full advantage of the autonomy allowed.[35] Sometimes charter leaders have difficulty balancing the role of instructional leader while managing the operation and finances of the school, as noted in a survey of a matched set of California charter and non-charter school principals.[36] Similarly, in a survey of four hundred charter leaders in North Carolina, school leaders reported challenges in addressing the issues of facilities, hiring teachers, and finances—all operational responsibilities in school leadership; 67 percent of this sample felt that they were not adequately prepared to lead a charter school.[37] As identified in interviews with six principals, the most difficult leadership tasks included providing effective leadership, completing the charter renewal process, and emergency dismissal due to unprofessional behavior.[38]

One way to respond to these challenges using the autonomy provided by the charter setting is to distribute leadership responsibilities. Based on a study of Milwaukee's charter and non-charter public schools from 1998 to 2002, Witte, Weimer, Shober, and Schlomer concluded that there were benefits to having two types of leaders: an inspirational person (or small group of individuals) to help start the school and shape its initial vision and then a competent, day-to-day administrator.[39] However, this distribution of leadership may be difficult, as Brown, Wohlstetter, and Liu found in their analysis of multiple academic and financial indicators of California charter schools, concluding that "charter schools compared to non-charter public schools tend to be light on administrative positions."[40]

Governing boards   Finally, the charter school governing board was an important autonomous actor in a charter school's decision making.[41] Unlike public school districts, where "big picture" decisions frequently lie with the elected school board, each charter school has the ability to identify and create a decision-making body that represents a range of stakeholders from the school community, including parents, teachers, and community members, among others.[42]

As indicated by a legislative review of charter laws and interviews with state charter leaders, states offer varying levels of autonomy to schools for how they set up their governing boards. As seen in table 4.3, charter school laws in twelve states require each charter school's governing board to include specific types of people (i.e., teachers, parents, or authorizer representatives) or have provisions concerning the maximum or minimum number of members.

TABLE 4.3

State requirements for charter school governing board composition

	Must have parents	Must have teachers	Minimum or maximum number of members	Must allow seat for authorizer	No relevant provisions
Alaska					X
Arizona					X
Arkansas					X
California				X	
Colorado					X
Connecticut	X	X			
Delaware	X	X			
District of Columbia	X		Max of 7		
Florida					X
Georgia					X
Hawaii	X	X			
Idaho					X
Illinois					X
Indiana					X
Iowa					X
Kansas					X
Louisiana					
Maryland					X
Massachusetts					X
Michigan					X
Minnesota		X	Min of 5		
Missouri					
Nevada		X			
New Hampshire	X				
New Jersey					X
New Mexico					X
New York					X

(continued)

TABLE 4.3 *(continued)*

State requirements for charter school governing board composition

	Must have parents	Must have teachers	Minimum or maximum number of members	Must allow seat for authorizer	No relevant provisions
North Carolina					X
Ohio			Min of 5		
Oklahoma					X
Oregon					X
Pennsylvania					X
Puerto Rico					X
Rhode Island					X
South Carolina		X*			
Tennessee	X				
Texas					X
Utah					X
Virginia	X**	X**			
Wisconsin					X
Wyoming					X

Source: Butler, Smith, and Wohlstetter, "Creating and sustaining high-quality charter school governing boards" (Los Angeles: National Resource Center for Finance and Governance, 2008).

* The law requires that teachers be part of the "charter committee," which is the founding governing body only "through the application process and until the election of a board of directors is held" (Section 59-40-40). There are no requirements that the operational board include teachers.

** Although Virginia's charter schools are under the jurisdiction of the local school district board, each school is required to have a "management committee" that includes parents and teachers.

However, creating and sustaining a high-quality board was a difficult challenge for two main reasons: recruiting an effective range of board members and ensuring that board members were trained and engaged in their responsibilities.[43] While a few state laws prescribed that certain types of board members (such as parents and teachers) sit on boards to broaden stakeholder participation, the majority of laws were silent on who should participate on a board. Additionally, laws have not generally required certain skill sets or mandated board training.[44]

One report examined charter school principals' perceptions of their governing boards.[45] Ninety percent or more of boards set a clear mission and high expectations, offered feedback, and tended not to micromanage. About half of the principals reported that their governing boards helped develop new sources of revenue, shielded the principal from controversies, and were involved in leadership succession. However, in case-study visits to twenty-four of these schools, only 25 percent of them "could accurately be described as active, critical, or making a positive impact in improving the schools."[46] The author concluded, "Given the central importance of governance to the charter school model, governing boards seem dramatically underutilized in many of these schools."[47]

QUESTIONS FOR THE FUTURE

Exactly how school-level autonomy—or its perception—influences student achievement has yet to be determined. One study found that two-thirds of charter school principals interviewed reported having autonomy in almost all areas was as necessary in raising student achievement, compared to fewer than one-third of non-charter school principals interviewed.[48] However, Zimmer and Buddin, in a study of California charters with a comparable set of non-charter schools based on propensity-score matching, concluded that "as with elementary and middle schools, the sharp differences in autonomy between charter schools and [non-charter publics] are not translating into differences in high school test scores."[49]

In reviewing past research on autonomy, a number of questions were raised.[50] First, are charters actually utilizing autonomy to bring about change, or is autonomy something that is granted but not used?[51] In looking across the various domains of schooling—the educational program, the school budget, and staffing—what levels of autonomy do charters need to succeed in each domain? Past research also suggests that although state laws grant charter schools autonomy, not all schools take advantage of this freedom to conduct school business in different and innovative ways; this finding leads to the issue of how to identify and react to potential barriers inhibiting autonomy.[52] The relationship between autonomy and accountability also needs further investigation, especially since the charter authorizing context and its emphasis on accountability have become more rigorous as the movement has matured.[53]

Finally, the relationship between autonomy and the growth of charter districts needs further exploration. The 93,000-student Fulton County school district in suburban Atlanta recently became a charter system, the largest system in Georgia (where sixteen districts hold charter status) to "charterize." A handful of other states allow charter districts—among them California, Florida, and New Mexico—and Texas allows groups to create a charter district from scratch as opposed to converting existing school districts. Todd Zeibarth of the National Alliance for Public Charter Schools wondered how much of the flexibility granted to charter districts would trickle down to schools: "I'm skeptical that the [charter] districts are freeing up their leaders at the school level. There's still kind of a top-down approach."[54]

CHAPTER FIVE

———■■■———

Have Charter Schools Provided Increased Opportunities for Parent Involvement?

FROM THE START, one of the core principles of the charter movement was to increase parent involvement in public schools. Parents who are dissatisfied with public schools could design and open their own charter school. This idea has played out "on the ground," as many charter schools are established by a founding group that includes parents. Parents, not the district, also play a large role in deciding which school their child will attend. The natural assumption flowing from this basic premise is that charter school parents, because they actively choose to send their child to a charter school, will be more involved than parents whose children are automatically assigned to a district-run school.[1] Charter schools also frequently involve parents in management roles, serving on governance boards or school committees, and there are instances of parents becoming members of the school staff as parent liaisons or as director of the school's parent center.

The goal of increased parent involvement is apparent when reviewing state charter legislation. For instance, Tennessee state legislators sought "to . . . afford parents substantial *meaningful opportunities* to participate in the education of their children."[2] Utah's charter school law stressed the importance of providing "opportunities for greater parental *involvement in management decisions* at the school level"[3] (emphasis added to both quotes).

It is clear that the legislative intent was that parent involvement in charter schools would go beyond bake sales and other fundraising activities. The charter reformers stressed involving parents not only for the good of their child but also to benefit the school organization. However, legislative intent does not erase the role that demographics play in a family's ability (and comfort level) to be involved in their child's education. White middle-class parents are traditionally the most visibly active in public schools.[4] Charter schools are not the first entity to attempt to change this fact. Federal policy through Title I of the Elementary and Secondary Education Act of 1965 has long mandated parent involvement in disadvantaged communities through parent advisory councils, but barriers continue to exist, particularly for urban, low-income, immigrant, minority, and working-class parents. Language barriers, work schedules, and a sense of disenfranchisement have generally resulted in lower levels of (at least visible) parent involvement by working-class parents, in particular, those from ethnic and racial minorities. While a growing body of research continues to advocate for parent involvement in urban schools as a key to increasing student performance, parent involvement in these schools remains elusive.[5]

Many charter schools are located in urban areas and disproportionately serve minority and low-income students (i.e., students qualifying for free or reduced-price lunch). The charter school movement is viewed by reformers as an opportunity for urban parents to play a more central role in the education of their children. Since charter schools have substantial decision-making autonomy, urban charters have been touted as settings in which the traditional barriers to parent involvement can be moderated. Unlike some large urban schools, charter schools are typically small "community schools" with missions tailored to their student populations. In addition, parents have the "right" to choose a school which makes accountability to the parent community more intense. Not surprisingly, there is an underlying assumption that charter schools involve more parents both quantitatively and qualitatively than non-charter public schools.

However, as different types of charter schools have evolved to include a range of schools, some have circumscribed the extent to which parents are involved. The Knowledge Is Power Program (KIPP), for instance, tends to feature a smaller role for parents. Parents who choose a KIPP school need to be comfortable with the school shaping the students' behavior, speaking patterns, and dress, in addition to student performance. Similarly, the SEED School, a public boarding school for sixth through twelfth grade, opened its doors in 1987. The school is founded on the belief that children in urban environments could benefit from an immersion program, which expressly limits parent involvement by having students live on campus Sunday through Friday.[6]

In this chapter, we delve into how parents are involved in charter schools and what some of the challenges have been. We start off with a brief look at what is known about the benefits of parent involvement to deepen our understanding of why charter reformers were so intent on increasing parents' roles. The goal of parent involvement shares some similarities with the goal of increasing community participation, which is discussed in chapter 2. Both goals seek to bring in and involve new players in public schools as a way to expand the expertise, knowledge, and skills to better serve the school's students.

WHY INVOLVE PARENTS?

Decades of research point to the numerous benefits of parent involvement in education not only for students but also for the parents, the school, and the wider community.[7] For example, research has found that parent involvement is related to a host of academic indicators, including grades, attendance, attitudes, expectations, homework completion, and state test results.[8] Additional academic outcomes such as lower dropout rates, fewer retentions, and fewer special education placements have been found as well.[9] Despite the challenges in establishing a causal link between parent involvement and student achievement, studies utilizing large databases have shown positive and statistically significant effects of parent involvement on both behavioral and academic outcomes.[10] Some researchers have found that only specific types of parent involvement appear to correlate with student achievement. These studies conclude that involvement at home, especially with parents discussing school activities and helping children plan their programs, appeared to have the strongest impact on academic achievement.[11] Other researchers found involvement at the school site made the key difference.[12]

In addition to academic outcomes, parent involvement also appears to have positive effects on students' behavior. Brody, Flor, and Gibson found that parenting practices contributed to students' increased ability to self-regulate their behavior.[13] Higher levels of social skills and improved overall behavior were also documented. In a study of American Indian students, researchers found that a parent intervention approach reduced students' disruptive behavior in the classroom; students were less aggressive and withdrawn after parent participation in the program.[14] Still other studies have documented the ways in which parent involvement supports children's social competencies in school.[15] Together, these studies and others suggest that parent involvement in schools can support student behavior and academic outcomes in schools, regardless of type.

TYPES AND FORMS OF PARENT INVOLVEMENT IN CHARTER SCHOOLS

Much of the research on parent involvement compares the level of involvement between charter and non-charter schools. For instance, a survey of principals in all California charter schools and a matched set of non-charter schools found that parent involvement was consistently higher at all grade levels in charters than in the matched counterparts.[16] Similarly, Mintrom's interviews with more than two hundred charter and non-charter school principals in Michigan found an average of 26 percent of parents regularly volunteered in the charter schools, compared with 20 percent of parents in other public schools. Further, 93 percent of the charter school principals included in the study reported that they attempted to create a school atmosphere that fostered parent involvement, compared with 75 percent of in the other schools.[17] These efforts manifested through a variety of mechanisms, including enrollment interviews, parent expectation surveys, and one-on-one principal-parent meetings. Mintrom concludes that parent involvement efforts were 9.4 percent more likely to be more innovative in charter than in non-charter schools.[18]

This innovative parent involvement has taken many forms, including involvement in school policy making by helping to write the charter school application or serving on the charter school's governing board.[19] For example, interviews with six charter school principals revealed that during the charter development phase, parents attended neighborhood and community meetings, gave input at public hearings, and in one case, provided recommendations through a parent advisory group regarding the establishment and focus of the school.[20]

Once a charter school is operational, innovative parent involvement includes creating new academic standards, aligning curriculum and assessments with the new standards, and transforming professional development. In one case, school administrators and teachers used the African-centered mission of a newly created charter school to involve parents in their child's education with the goal of improved academic achievement as well as other positive social outcomes. Certain school events, such as rites of passage, field trips, and volunteer events, focused on involving parents. The school also used parents as role models in their various character-building activities to promote ethical character development, discipline, responsibility, and accountability.[21]

Parent involvement roles also included fulfilling school needs by volunteering in the school office, serving as crossing guards, participating in school beautification projects, or driving the school bus.[22] In many cases parents were involved in budgetary decisions; data from the 1999–2000 Schools and Staffing Survey (SASS) found that 50.1 percent of the charter schools invited parents to participate in budget decisions, compared to 44.9 percent of the non-charter public schools and 36.4 percent of the private schools.[23]

Mintrom found that charter schools achieved greater parent participation through the use of parent contracts, which were used in 37 percent of charter schools in the study, compared with 22 percent of non-charter schools. The author also identified the use of preenrollment informational interviews, used by 68 percent of the charter schools, compared with 34 percent of non-charter schools, to boost parent participation.[24]

In a more recent study of twelve urban charter schools in six states, Smith, Kuzin, De Pedro, and Wohlstetter found that the strategies used to implement parent involvement activities and to attract hard-to-reach parents were fairly innovative. Study schools offered wrap-around services, incentives, and contracts to enhance and ensure participation; utilized technology for advertising parent volunteer opportunities; and involved parents in the decision making and governance of the school.[25] Overall, these strategies were perceived by school officials to be linked to improving parents' self-efficacy and comfort level in participating in their child's education.

Challenges remain, however, when it comes to involving a diverse set of parents. The simple act of choosing to send one's child to a charter school may not indicate a commitment to get involved at the school, on the one hand, or knowledge of how to do so, on the other. Indeed, studies suggest that parents choose schools for a whole host of reasons, including the ethnic, racial, or economic demographics of the school, availability of transportation options, or lack of access to other educational options.[26]

QUESTIONS FOR THE FUTURE

Parental involvement has been shown to be higher in charter schools than in non-charter schools, with parents involved in a variety of school roles including policy making, budgetary decisions, and providing academic input. Although many charter schools strive to achieve high levels of parent involvement in line with state goals, not all parents have access to the same level of information in order to make informed educational choices. Certain groups of parents, as from non-English-speaking or low-income families, may not have full access to information. Policy makers can increase access of information to parents and help engage parents in collaborative relationships with schools. Outreach of this nature could help states and districts meet the goal of providing more options to all families by providing additional support and outreach, particularly to those who are least advantaged or in failing schools.

Policy makers should also consider parental choice motivations and behaviors when designing school choice policies in order to address the varied motivations driving parent actions. We also see evidence that charter school operators are likewise responding to parental motivations. Take, for example, charter management organizations that have opened more schools and expanded grade levels in direct response to parent demand in the communities they serve. Establishing a market or demand from families for a new charter school as part of the initial application may be one way to directly link school choice policies with parental motivations and behaviors.

A significant body of research is dedicated to understanding parents' preferences and reported motivations in making school choice decisions for their children. However, there is much less research around parent behavior—what they actually do—and how it relates to reported preferences. Another area of unanswered questions about parent involvement in charters concerns what factors facilitate or inhibit parents from making school choices based on their preferences, including whether or not districts ensure access and equity for all parents to a variety of education providers. There is also the issue of parent contracts—how are they being implemented, and do they serve to cream charter school applicants or to educate families about parent involvement?

Finally, the general consensus up to now is that more parent involvement is better than less. However, we know little about the differential effects of various types of parent involvement. Could it be that not all types of parent involvement are equally good? Is it possible that some types of parent involvement are associated with negative effects on parents and students?

CHAPTER SIX

———■■■———

Have Charter Schools
Been Subject to
Increased Accountability?

IN THE HALLS OF STATE CAPITOLS, charter school champions wooed potential supporters by emphasizing that charter schools were the new and improved version of an earlier education reform—community participation and school-based management. Beginning in the 1960s and through the 1980s, decentralization reforms received considerable attention across the United States from a wide range of states and school districts.[1] The good thing about these decentralization reforms, argued the charter champions, was that they pushed decision making about education programs, staffing, and the budget down to individual school communities. Through school-based management, those closest to students were empowered to make decisions that could then be tailored to meet the needs of the students.

The new twist that the charter school movement brought was accountability. With decentralized decision making in the earlier era, there were few, if any, consequences for making wrong or bad decisions. Charter reformers stressed that charter schools would be

different. While the school community was empowered with decision-making authority, there also would be consequences. First,
charter schools would be schools of choice: families who were dissatisfied with the school could switch to a different school, and
the public "tuition" dollars would follow the student to the new
school. Second, charter schools would operate under a performance
contract. In crafting their charter school laws, states decided who
would have the authority to approve, monitor, and renew or revoke
the performance contract. State legislatures also would decide the
length of the contract period, which turned out to range from three
to fifteen years, with most states opting for three- to five-year contracts. In sum, a big difference between charter schools and the
earlier decentralized schools was that the charters of schools that
did not meet the terms of their performance contracts would be
revoked, and the schools closed down.

As the charter movement has evolved over the past twenty
years, the rhetoric emphasizing "autonomy in exchange for
accountability" has remained steady, but the reality of implementation has been challenging. In this chapter, we discuss some of the
challenges to upholding the original agreement. In considering the
research focusing on accountability and charter schools, we find
something different than what the reformers had envisioned. To a
great extent, bureaucratic accountability—compliance with rules
and regulations—has often taken the place of performance or market accountability.

We begin the chapter with an orientation to the various types
of accountability, drawing from charter school laws and research
on school accountability. Most recently, attention has been placed
on ensuring high-quality charters, a move to counter the reality
that most charter schools close because of financial or governance
issues, not because of low academic performance. As such, most
of the chapter is devoted to the role of charter authorizers—the
accountability enforcers—examining who they are, how they have
taken on this responsibility, and the extent to which charter schools
have indeed been held accountable.

CHARTER SCHOOL ACCOUNTABILITY:
RHETORIC VERSUS REALITY

The goal of increased or new measures of accountability is mentioned in twenty-seven state laws. Turning to the charter school laws themselves, we see that lawmakers across states had different notions of accountability in mind. Some states had a broad understanding of accountability. In Indiana, for instance, legislators aspired to "allow public schools freedom and flexibility in exchange for exceptional levels of accountability."[2] Charter laws from other states, such as Minnesota and New York, specifically emphasized an increased attention to accountability grounded in student and school performance. California's charter law, for example, aims to "hold the schools established under this part accountable for meeting measurable pupil outcomes, and provide the schools with a method to change from rule-based to performance-based accountability systems."[3] And still others focused on the accountability that would develop as part of the newly created market of schools that included both charter and non-charter public schools. In Florida, the law includes the provision that charter schools will "provide rigorous competition within the public school district to stimulate continual improvement in all public schools."[4] Indeed, within and across charter laws, accountability has been multifaceted.

Traditionally in education, accountability and student achievement were only loosely connected. Assessment was mainly used for diagnostic purposes or for dividing students into ability-based groups. Accountability, on the other hand, was of the political sort, as reflected in elected boards' accountability to local constituents. Schools were accountable to district administrators, who, in turn, were accountable to elected boards.

Now, since the advent of standards-based reform and more recent federal legislation, including No Child Left Behind and Race to the Top, accountability and student achievement have become more closely linked. In this new view of accountability, content and performance standards are aligned with a curriculum and set of assessments that measure successful attainment of those standards. Eventually, the assessment results lead to consequences—rewards or sanctions that introduce incentives for improvement. Current state and federal accountability systems feature the use of student testing to measure school performance in order to reward schools that achieve their standards or to sanction schools that fall short. This type of accountability is known as standards- or performance-based accountability.[5] For charter schools, the expectation is that schools will be closed if they are failing to meet high academic achievement goals.[6]

Performance-based accountability stands in contrast with bureaucratic accountability. Under bureaucratic accountability, schools or districts need to comply with regulations and procedures delineated and monitored by external authorities. In other words, bureaucratic accountability involves "the adherence to rules and regulations put forth by a governing body," including federal, state, and local governments, and in the case of charter schools, their authorizing body.[7] Authorizers all address the same basic issues: evaluating and approving applications, overseeing the school during the contract period, and deciding whether to renew or revoke the charter when the chartering period ends. With the closures of charter schools occurring mostly due to governance and fiscal management issues, one might conclude that this type of accountability has superseded the others, mainly because the accountability decisions with regard to bureaucratic accountability are far more black-and-white than with performance accountability.

Market accountability—related to economic market theory, choice, and supply and demand—involves accountability to the customers of charter schools, namely, the parents and students. Underlying this source of accountability is the principle that parents and students can choose the school that best fits their needs, that is, that provides the highest quality educational services. If a school fails to meet the needs of the school community, the parents and students have the option to "vote with their feet," change schools, and bring their per-pupil funding with them. Furthermore, a marketplace of employment options is also created for teachers, administrators, and staff. If staff members are not happy with their work environment at a particular school, they can choose to apply to work at other schools. In theory, as schools of choice, charter schools must meet the needs of their "customers" by providing a superior academic program or else face being closed because of low enrollment and/or staffing problems.[8]

Finally, professional accountability is based on educators feeling accountable to their peers and professional associations for following recognized professional practices. Professional accountability may occur formally as recognition through professional honors, through sanctions, or through the receipt or loss of certification. It may also occur more informally as educators create internal accountability within an organization through setting and meeting standards of practice. In both cases, professional accountability is aimed at advancing increased knowledge and skills, collaboration, and trust, leading to increased organizational capacity, and, ultimately, to improved school and student performance. (For further information concerning professional accountability, please see chapter 1 for the discussion of new roles for teachers.)

One point looms large for charter advocates. Despite the intention that performance-based accountability will lead to the closure of poor performing schools, in fact, most charter schools close because of financial mismanagement or problems with their governance—that is, in response to bureaucratic accountability. In a recent report, the Center on Education Reform announced that of the roughly 6,700 charter schools that have opened in the United States, 15 percent have closed. Of those that have closed, 41.7 percent have gone under for financial reasons, with organizational mismanagement as the next most likely reason at 24 percent. Closure because of poor academic performance only occurred 18.6 percent of the time.[9]

Subsequently, there has been greater emphasis on higher-quality chartering instead of the prior tenet of "Let every flower bloom." Rather than just depending on accountability forces to eventually shut down lower performing schools, this new push includes growing roles for those involved in the charter sector to ensure high-quality education. Charter authorizers are increasingly being recognized as key players in this work.

AUTHORIZERS' ROLES IN HOLDING CHARTER SCHOOLS ACCOUNTABLE

Charter school authorizers are the organizations with the legal authority to grant and revoke charters. Recent research has shown that not all authorizers are created or operate equally; while they all may share similar responsibilities, there is wide variation in the different types and approaches. While authorizers are intended to be the "gatekeepers" of quality, this role has proven to be difficult, especially when balancing demands of school autonomy and performance-based accountability.

Who is Tasked with Enforcing Charter School Accountability?

As shown in figure 6.1, the types of organizations that authorize charter schools vary according to state law and may include local and state school boards, special charter boards, higher education institutions, nonprofit organizations, or city or mayor's offices.[10]

In many cases, it is the local school district or state board of education that serves as authorizer. One study that surveyed 860 state and charter officials and operators in twenty-four states found that local education agencies have had a difficult time with their role as authorizer because they are "most influenced by charter-averse interest groups and often did not have adequate infrastructure to support authorizing activities."[11]

Another study suggested that the number of authorizers, regardless of type, was less important than the authorizer's capacity and dedication to their authorizing tasks.[12] Palmer found in her interviews and surveys that alternative authorizers—such as independent state-level charter boards, higher education institutions, nonprofit institutions, and municipal offices—have been effective authorizers because of their desire to be authorizers, their relative isolation from politics, and their ability to develop additional infrastructure for performance-based accountability. The author argues

FIGURE 6.1

Percentage of charter schools by type of authorizer: 2009–10 school year

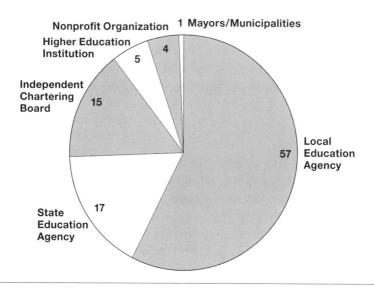

Source: National Association of Charter School Authorizers (NACSA) "State-by-State Overview" (Chicago: 2010).

that the best authorizers, regardless of their type, want the job, insulate themselves sufficiently from politics to do the job well, and have the money and other tools they need to focus on quality. However, alternative authorizers often have a stronger desire than traditional authorizers to get involved in chartering and can base their decisions on data rather than politics. When provided with adequate funding, alternative authorizers can secure staff members and create systems focused on outcomes rather than on compliance with rules.[13]

What Are the Accountability Enforcement Responsibilities of Authorizers?

Authorizers fill a variety of roles during the life cycle of a charter school; at each stage of the cycle they can play a role in identifying, supporting, and rewarding performance, and, in some cases, in enforcing performance accountability and closing schools. Authorizers can encourage the development of a supply of quality charter school providers, often done through a request for proposals publicized on their Web site. Through the application process, authorizers screen and select operators. After granting a charter, they are then responsible for overseeing and monitoring the school's performance and holding charter schools accountable for meeting their performance targets through to charter renewal or revocation.[14]

Developing applicants and reviewing applications   In case studies of eight "high-quality" authorizers in multiple states, Public Impact and WestEd described how authorizers actively develop a talent pool of potential operators, through "strategic recruitment locally and nationally for charter school operators that show strong potential for being successful."[15] After attracting applications, often done through a request for proposals publicized on their Web site, authorizers are responsible for reviewing the applications, a first step in ensuring that only those with a strong plan, vision, and mission for a charter school receive charters. In a review of early literature on authorizer research, Bulkley suggests that early on in the charter movement, authorizers might have been ill-prepared for the responsibilities associated with reviewing charter applications. However, as they have gained more experience, authorizers have become better equipped: "Since those early years, authorizers with more experience have developed clearer guidelines for applicants, and in some cases, clearer guidelines for the evaluation of applications."[16] Public Impact and WestEd describe how "high-quality" authorizers identify and select operators based on a clear and transparent process that involves demonstrated community support and multiple measures for evaluating operator potential.[17]

Monitoring the charter agreement   In terms of oversight, research suggests that effective, performance-based charter school oversight was time-consuming but best accomplished when there were solid relationships, multiple sources of information, and regular site visits.[18] However, authorizers sometimes got bogged down with red tape and compliance-centered practices rather than emphasizing performance-based outcomes.[19] For example, in their surveys of charter operators, authorizers, and state special education officials in twenty-four states, Lange, Rhim, and Ahearn note the importance of authorizers in helping schools understand and be accountable for special education regulations.[20]

The final role of an authorizer is in the charter renewal or revocation process. The decision to close a charter school is difficult because of the social and economic costs, political opposition, practical difficulties, negative community response, potential legal constraints, and harmful backlash to the larger charter movement.[21] As Vergari further explains, "as constituencies build in support of a given charter school, and as [authorizers] engage in friendly relations with the schools they have authorized, it may be difficult to close a charter school that is not meeting high standards."[22] Bulkley refers to the challenges around closure as the "accountability bind, as authorizers are stuck between wanting to enforce accountability through renewal, but finding doing so fraught with difficulty."[23]

Authorizers face a variety of challenges in performing these responsibilities. First, authorizers may have insufficient organizational resources to efficiently and effectively manage their responsibilities. Another challenge relates to vestiges of political ill will toward the charter sector, or, as Palmer and Gau explain, "many state policy environments [are] not supportive of charter schools and authorizers."[24] Additionally, authorizers often struggle with balancing performance-based accountability of their schools, expectations for school-level autonomy and flexibility, and the development and support of a diverse charter market.[25]

Authorizers have had different styles or approaches to their responsibilities. For instance, some have had a "hands-on" or "proactive, assistance-oriented" relationship with their schools, as noted in a qualitative study of eleven statewide authorizers in

Arizona, Massachusetts, and Michigan that included interviews and document analysis.[26] Those authorizers who wanted to build trust between the authorizer and their charter schools or to promote learning across schools adopted this style. Other authorizers had an "arms-length" or "legalistic" approach based on the philosophic belief that it was not the role of the authorizer to encroach on school autonomy.[27]

Researchers have identified a series of characteristics that "successful" authorizers share. For instance, Palmer and Gau both note that a relative insulation from politics, coupled with an ability to make data-driven decisions, allowed authorizers to make decisions based on quality rather than political considerations.[28] In their profiles of eight authorizers, Public Impact and WestEd highlighted six best practices for high performing authorizers. These authorizers "build a strong [internal] organization, develop a strong talent pool, select [operators] for quality, support new school operators, provide meaningful and transparent oversight, [and] hold schools accountable for meeting performance goals."[29]

QUESTIONS FOR THE FUTURE

A fair assumption is that charter school operators, authorizers, and policy makers do not want low performing schools to continue, as it taints the larger charter movement and their own reform efforts. As the movement has aged, the public—at least in the abstract—may be getting more comfortable with performance-based accountability and closing down low achieving schools. The federal No Child Left Behind Act, for instance, included several options for restarting or closing down schools with chronic low performance. In a possible signal of a greater emphasis on performance-based accountability in the future, the New York City Department of Education moved to close down Peninsula Preparatory Charter School for its consistently mediocre scores on the city's progress reports in January 2012. The *New York Times* article on the event reported that many education advocates see this move as a "warning to schools that it is no longer sufficient to be as good as or slightly better than traditional public schools; they have to be exemplars."[30]

Many agree that accountability among schools of choice needs to be more strictly enforced.[31] Charter schools are built on the bargain of greater autonomy for more accountability; if schools are not performing well, they need to be closed.[32] State laws could be adapted to attract higher-quality charter operators and to place pressure on authorizers to close low performing schools.[33] More recently, states have given consideration to beefing up the authorizer side of the equation by requiring that organizations *apply* to be designated charter school authorizers, rather than be entitled to the position based on provisions in the state charter law.

This mind shift has been led, in part, by the efforts of the National Association of Charter School Authorizers (NACSA) to instill in authorizers that they need to take seriously their oversight functions, including closing down charter schools if they are not meeting their performance targets. NACSA's mission statement—"to achieve the establishment and operation of quality charter schools through responsible oversight in the public interest"—suggests that quality charter authorizing leads to greater numbers of quality charter schools. In their role as advocate for quality authorizers, NACSA in 2004 released its first edition of *Principles and Standards for Quality Charter School Authorizing*, which reflected lessons learned by experienced authorizers. The NACSA document is used to guide authorizing practices: "The Principles articulate a set of beliefs about quality charter school authorizing. The Standards identify core authorizer responsibilities and describe how the principles are upheld within each core responsibility." More recently, NACSA's assistance has included customized services for authorizer development, and in fall 2012, NACSA will launch the Institute for Leadership in Charter School Authorizing.

The central challenge for state and district policy makers is to balance this call for added accountability with honoring school-level autonomy.[34] As Bulkley and Hicks note, "districts must struggle with how to support building-level autonomy while aiding schools in developing a strong sense of mission and powerful professional community."[35] Policy makers will also want to consider the types of accountability mechanisms they have in place: bureaucratic, performance, and market.[36] Overreliance on one kind of accountability may lead to unintended consequences. Focusing on performance measures alone may lead schools to narrow their curriculum, while depending on market mechanisms may encourage schools to devote time to improving marketing campaigns rather than school quality.[37] Garn and Cobb suggest that states "blend multiple models of accountability [to] better inform all constituents—including parents and taxpayers—about the performance of publicly funded schools."[38]

—■■■—

CHAPTER SEVEN

What Have Been the Results of Charter School Competition?

AS NOTED IN THE INTRODUCTION, charter schools when first introduced were not an entirely new innovation. Instead, the reform known as charter schools represented tinkering with a package of reforms that had been tested out individually in the past. In particular, the notion of school choice, with schools competing with one another to attract and retain students, was originally proposed in the 1950s by the late University of Chicago economist and Nobel Laureate Milton Friedman. Friedman's political philosophy was grounded in libertarianism and the Republican Party. He advocated strongly against monopolies of public services. Instead he extolled the virtues of a free market system, with little intervention by government and with service providers competing for "consumers." In his 1955 article "The Role of Government in Education," Friedman proposed supplementing publicly operated schools with privately run but publicly funded schools through a system of school vouchers.

While some countries, such as Chile and Sweden, adopted the voucher idea nationally, the idea did not take hold as rapidly or pervasively in the United States. It was not until over a decade later, in the early 1970s, that the Alum Rock Union Elementary School District serving students from K–8 in San Jose, California, under a grant from the federal Office of Economic Opportunity, ran the first voucher experiment, aimed at giving all families in the district a choice of school options.[1] The experiment was not much of a success, largely because many families did not exercise their right to choose a different school but instead remained at their local school. Subsequent voucher programs in a few jurisdictions (the District of Columbia, Indiana, Louisiana, Milwaukee, and Ohio, as of October 2011) tended to target specific student populations—poor students, special education students, or students who were not being well served by their home school. [2] Nevertheless, while voucher programs have continued sporadically for decades in the United States, they have been more of a sideshow than the main attraction in school reform, largely because of the political baggage associated with the term. For example, in California, the charter school law was proposed at the same time as a voucher initiative; the charter school bill won out.[3]

It was not until the first charter school law passed in Minnesota that traces of Friedman's free market ideas resurfaced in a significant way. Charter school proponents argued that if per-pupil funding flowed to the school a student attended, schools would compete with one another to attract and retain students, and this would lead to a stronger education system. As additional states passed charter laws, many of them included the intention for charters to have spillover effects, causing improvements not only in charter schools but in non-charter public schools as well. Charter reformers envisioned charter schools competing with district-run schools, and also charter schools competing against one another. Competition in education invested market participants—families shopping for schools for their children—with the authority to select a school on their own, unregulated by government. Charter schools that were selected by families and were in demand would survive;

those that were not would either re-create themselves or go out of existence.

Policy champions imagined that individual charter schools would be created in sufficient numbers that eventually—one school at a time—charters would reach the tipping point where districts would be forced to improve practices to compete for students. It was also expected that districts would replicate in other public schools those charter education programs that were in high demand. Systemic change would occur as more charters opened and as non-charter schools adopted new education programs; students would have more schooling options which, in turn, would improve achievement for all students in the district.

In the early years of the charter school movement, researchers looked for instances of districts' replication of charter programs, but the evidence was spotty and anecdotal. In a pioneering study that examined how public school districts in eight states were responding to charter schools, the report concluded that with rare exceptions, school districts were largely ignoring charters.[4] Rofes went on to cite a few examples of school districts that were inspired by charter schools to make mild and moderate efforts to "out-charter the charters" and replicate their educational programs, including all-day kindergartens in Lansing, Michigan, and Mesa, Arizona; thematic schools in Boston, Denver, and Grand Rapids, Michigan; and a Montessori-based program in Rochester, Minnesota. This early study made it clear that the threat of charters at this point, either to one another or to district-run schools, was mild. There just were not enough charter schools being opened in sufficient concentration to force schools to close or reinvent themselves.

However, times have changed. In their sixth annual report on charter school market share, the National Alliance for Public Charter Schools reported that in the 2010–2011 school year, six districts had at least 30 percent of their public school students enrolled in charter schools, with New Orleans topping the list at 70 percent.[5] Nearly a hundred districts nationwide have 10 percent of their students attending charter schools, considered by some to be the tipping point to cause districts to evaluate their own practices.

As Cannata notes, "The mechanism through which the competitive effects of charter schools are assumed to work depends on the perceptions and actions of non-charter school personnel. That is, to be motivated to act, school personnel must perceive as detrimental the threat or actuality of losing students to charter schools."[6]

Manifestations of a competitive effect would likely be seen in four areas: 1) an impact (negative or positive) on the performance of students remaining in non-charter public schools; 2) a change in the behavior of teachers, school leaders, and/or district administrators in response to the perceived competition; 3) spillover effects in which district-run schools mimic education programs in charters; and 4) increased financial efficiency of achieving desired education outcomes, which is included as a specific goal in one state law. This chapter explores each of these in turn.

EFFECTS OF CHARTER SCHOOL COMPETITION ON THE PERFORMANCE OF NON-CHARTER PUBLIC SCHOOL STUDENTS

Competition from successful charter schools could affect the performance of students remaining in non-charter schools in several ways. On the most basic level, if charter schools are "skimming" the highest performing students from other public schools, a reasonable assumption would be that the students left behind would be lower performing, resulting in lower test scores for these schools. Alternatively, if charter schools serve at-risk or low performing students, the opposite can be assumed to result. Beyond simply changing the population of students being served by non-charter schools, competition posed by the establishment of charter schools in an area could affect the performance of students in the other schools. Theory posits that one way charter schools could do this is if charters act as "laboratories of innovation," wherein new approaches are piloted and the successful ones then adopted by districts and states; however, studies have shown little evidence of this.[7] Another scenario hypothesizes that the competition created by charter schools will impel non-charter schools to improve;

in this view, charter schools will serve as a "rising tide that lifts all boats." One challenge to this theory is that there is a "tension between competition, which may put charter schools at odds with district-run public schools, and 'borrowing ideas,' which requires a more collaborative relationship."[8]

Considering these contradictory assumptions, it is not surprising that the impact of charter presence on the achievement of students in surrounding schools or districts has been mixed. A number of studies have found evidence that the presence of charter schools had a positive influence on student achievement more broadly.[9] Stoddard and Kuhn, for example, found that the presence of charter school laws had a positive influence on fourth-grade National Assessment of Educational Progress (NAEP) scores in math, particularly in states with "strong" charter school laws.[10] Ladner found that the academic gains of Tucson-area public schools facing competition were approximately 5.4 times larger in reading and twice as large in math as the comparison group of schools facing no competition.[11] Booker, Gilpatric, Gronberg, and Jansen analyzed the impact of charter competition on particular subgroups in Texas and found that the presence of charter schools increased the performance of students remaining behind in other public schools for African American and Hispanic students as well as for students at low performing schools.[12] Using district-level data from Texas over multiple years, Bohte found that the presence and growth of charter schools had a moderately positive impact on overall student pass rates at non-charter schools and also positively influenced the passage rates on state tests of low-income students.[13] The author hypothesized that this improvement in passing rates at non-charter schools was due to either of two factors: 1) policy changes initiated by district administrators in an attempt to curb the loss of funding caused by students electing to attend charter schools (higher pass rates on state tests, for example, could have been used to attract parents back to the regular schools), or 2) the "reverse creaming" movement of at-risk students from non-charter schools to charters. In this second scenario, administrators in non-charter schools "purposely encourage the transfer of weaker students to charter schools in order to focus on less resource-intensive student populations."[14]

In other cases, research has found little or no evidence of charter schools improving the achievement of students in the broader public education system.[15] In some studies, the presence of charter schools has been shown to reduce test score gains in nearby schools, a finding that supports the notion that charter schools "skim" the best students from other public schools.[16] For example, Bifulco and Ladd found that in North Carolina, competition from charter schools reduced student reading score gains in schools located within 2.5 miles of a charter school and had no effect on gains in schools located between 2.5 and 10 miles from a charter school.[17] There was no effect one way or the other on math scores. In another case, Ni found that charter school competition in Michigan had a negative impact on both fourth- and seventh-grade test scores—0.2 standard deviations in math and 0.4 to 0.5 standard deviations in reading.[18] Using a pooled time series regression analysis of Ohio schools, Carr and Ritter found that charter school competition had a small, negative effect on the proficiency passage rates of non-charter schools located in the same district.[19]

In an attempt to unpack the different findings regarding the impact of charter schools on systemwide student achievement, Arsen and Ni reviewed a set of studies.[20] The authors concluded that "the weight of the research suggests that charter school competition is not a very consistent force in its impact on [non-charter public schools'] achievement in one way or another." The authors hypothesized that the variation in results may stem from differences in the following three areas:[21]

- *Research methods:* The units of analysis varied across the studies, but there was no clear link between findings that use student-level versus school- or district-level data. For instance, Imberman used three different quantitative models—school fixed-effects, school fixed-effects with school-specific time trends, and instrumental variables—to assess the impact of charter schools on student behavior, attendance, and test scores in the surrounding district; he found different results depending on the methodological approach used.[22]

- *State charter school policies:* Charter schools in states in which the full per-pupil allocation followed the student were expected to exert a negative impact on non-district charter school test scores, if districts have no way to make up for the lost revenue.

- *State settings:* The pace of overall enrollment growth or decline may have influenced whether competitive effects were positive or negative, depending on whether charter school enrollments helped alleviate overcrowding or left non-charter district schools short on resources.[23]

EFFECTS OF CHARTER SCHOOL COMPETITION ON THE BEHAVIOR OF TEACHERS, SCHOOL LEADERS, AND DISTRICT ADMINISTRATORS

The response by teachers, school leaders, and district administrators to the competition created by the presence of charter schools has also varied over time and by location, with some studies identifying specific behavioral responses to the perceived competition. For example, a review of the first decade of charter school research reported on a study of twenty-five school districts across eight states and the District of Columbia and found that districts enacted peripheral changes in response to charter school competition: "Common responses to the presence of charter schools included increasing marketing and public relations efforts."[24]

The existence of charter schools was seen to affect the behavior of teachers in schools systemwide. Stoddard and Kuhn's analysis data from the 1987, 1990, 1993, and 1999 Schools and Staffing Survey found that the number of hours worked by teachers systemwide increases along with both the percentage of students in a state enrolled in charters and the number of years the law has been in place.[25]

Another early study in Arizona found more significant reactions to the competitive pressures presented by the charter schools in the district: three of the four case-study districts profiled in the study "changed district superintendents in the study period and the fourth nearly did so," which was attributed in part to charter competition.[26] In addition to changes in superintendent leadership, the school districts made changes relative to district size and resources, the growth or decline of the charter market, the student populations targeted by the charter schools, and the perceived quality of the charter schools.

Through interviews with eight urban superintendents in Ohio, May uncovered three common themes in reaction to the competition created by charter schools:[27]

- Their roles as superintendents changed to include marketing schools to the public, a responsibility they were ill equipped to take on.
- The school choice movement, and especially charter schools, negatively affected urban public schools disproportionately.
- Superintendents needed to make changes to "reclaim" students who had left traditional public schools in favor of schools of choice. This required "district-wide, long-term initiatives with commitment among all levels of the organization, from the school secretary's smile to the returned phone call from the superintendent."[28]

More recently, Zimmer and Buddin's survey of non-charter public school principals from across California found that 21.4 percent of school leaders statewide and 40 percent of principals in six districts with significant charter enrollments reported instituting reforms in response to the presence of charter schools.[29] Changes included altering compensation structures, teacher hiring and firing policies, curriculum and instructional practices, and professional development.

EFFECTS OF CHARTER SCHOOL COMPETITION ON EDUCATION PROGRAMS

Spillover effects in which district-run schools mimic education programs in charters (e.g., longer school day / longer school year) have surfaced in recent years. The degree to which research has observed spillover effects in non-charter schools and school districts has varied over time and by location. In an early survey of charter school and school district leaders in North Carolina, O'Sullivan, Nagle, and Spence found that the majority of district leaders and charter school heads reported no change (and anticipated no expected change in the future) in programs offered, redistribution of administrative time, or parent concerns.[30]

A 2003 study in Minnesota concluded that the presence of charter schools led to the creation of small alternative schools and regional learning centers for at-risk students. Interviewees reported that these district actions followed the realization "that if they did not create such options, teachers would simply create charters."[31] Parents also played a role in district responses to the passage of the charter school law. When parents threatened to use the charter school law to open a Montessori charter school, the district agreed to work with parents to create a district-run Montessori school.

Competition can also occur among charter schools. One large study that examined 1,147 charter school applications from 1991 to 1998 in twenty-nine states found "a competitive process between extant charter schools in a district and the initiation of future schools."[32] The author concluded that in effect, charters competed with one another: an increase in the number of existing charter schools led to a decrease in the number of charter school applications submitted. However, it was also possible that, in some states with already large populations of charter schools, the existence of caps acted as a limiting factor.

EFFECTS OF CHARTER SCHOOL COMPETITION ON FINANCIAL EFFICIENCY

Charter schools have generally not increased the financial efficiency of achieving desired education outcomes. Rather, financial challenges remain one of the most common reasons for charter school closures. Despite this, limited research suggests that the autonomy granted to charter schools has produced some cost-effective ways of educating students, as mentioned in chapter 4. Grosskopf, Hayes, and Taylor compared student achievement gains with school inputs in urban charter and non-charter schools in Texas and found that, of the two, charter schools were substantially more efficient.[33] The authors hypothesized that charter schools' efficiency was due to freedom from many of the regulations governing the operation of non-charter schools; for example, as noted in chapter 4:

- Non-charter schools in the state were required to have a maximum pupil-teacher ratio of 22 to 1 in grades K–3; charter schools faced no such maximum.
- Non-charter schools were required to have counselors and a nurse beyond a specified minimum student enrollment; charter schools were exempt from this requirement.
- The state-mandated minimum salary scale did not apply to charter schools.

Although it might be assumed that for-profit, EMO charter schools would be more efficient, Hill and Welsch's study of charter schools in Michigan found no evidence of this.[34] In terms of financial efficiency, one study tackled the question of how charters compared to other reforms. Yeh assessed the hypothetical relative cost of realizing student achievement gains through five different reforms: charters, vouchers, improvements in testing systems, a 10-percent increase in per-pupil expenditures, and increased accountability.[35] The author found that the implementation of a testing system that provided feedback to teachers and students on student performance in math and reading two to five times a week (called "rapid assessment") was 64 times more effective than charter schools in improving student achievement. The author calculated that the achievement gains per dollar from rapid assessment are 23,166 times the gains that accrue from charter schools.

At the same time, some studies have shown that the competition created by charter schools has had a negative financial impact on regular public schools. In one study, over half of the respondents reported a financial impact, with district leaders expressing serious concerns about the financial implications of charter schools in their districts. Contrary to this, one study of principals statewide compared to the six districts with significant charter enrollments found that more than 80 percent of principals reported that the presence of charter schools "had no effect on financial security, the ability to acquire necessary resources, teacher recruitment and retention, and the ability to attract and retain students at their school."[36]

QUESTIONS FOR THE FUTURE

Charter schools are frequently only one part of a larger system of public school choice that can include traditional public schools, magnet schools, homeschooling, and vouchers, among others. In recent years, the portfolio approach has taken hold in several large urban school districts (e.g., Chicago, Denver, Los Angeles, and New York) such that the providers of schooling and the choices offered to families are far broader than they once were.[37] Past research suggests that choice mechanisms work differently depending on the school model; for instance, magnet schools use selective criteria, while charters use lottery systems. This differing access to schools of choice may affect competitive outcomes.[38] One author suggests that the "limitations imposed by the charter school structure may dampen the effects of competition sufficiently that there will be a lack of empirical evidence demonstrating the gains to be had from truly reforming our public school system."[39] Indeed, Imberman suggests that "if charters are to be an effective strategy for improving student performance, there would need to be a large enough supply [of charter schools] so that students could attend charters throughout their entire academic careers."[40] Future research can consider the mechanism of competition—for charters specifically and for public schools more generally—within these changing and evolving portfolio models.

Second, another issue looking forward is the diversity of parents and what is known about who chooses to attend a charter school. Consider findings from the original voucher experiment in Alum Rock that have since been echoed in recent studies. The threat of competition that undergirds the charter movement will probably not be realized until charter schools find ways to communicate more effectively to parents—all parents—that they have a choice of where to send their children, and until those parents have the information and knowledge to make informed decisions.

On the flip side, recent anecdotal evidence suggests an uptick of charter-district collaboration. Some of these relationships are fueled by philanthropic organizations. For example, the Bill and Melinda Gates Foundation in 2010 began an initiative for districts to work with charter schools. The District-Charter Collaboration Compact, which has sixteen districts signed on to work with charter schools, is trying to get beyond relationships of isolation and antagonism.[41] In one Compact school district, the Sacramento City Unified School District in California, the Emerging Leaders Academy brings together district schools and charter schools for joint principal leadership training—twenty people from the district and twenty from charters.[42] As part of New York City's District-Charter Collaboration Compact, NYC Collaborates was set up as an initiative to address issues of parity between the district and charter schools, including "enrollment, funding, facilities and data . . . [to] encourage replication of high-performing models, most importantly, [to] improve and expand the ways in which district and charters work together and influence each other for the benefit of all students in the city."[43]

In addition to the work of foundations, there are examples of district-charter collaboration starting organically from within school districts or by place-based intermediary organizations.

- Synergy Charter Academy in Los Angeles entered into an agreement with the Los Angeles School Board to share space with a new non-charter district school. The founders of Synergy were considering moving one of its campuses out of a cramped church space. Hearing that the Los Angeles Unified School District (LAUSD) was opening up a new non-charter school about a block away, they approached LAUSD administrators and board members to see if Synergy could share space with the new school, share best practices with its teacher and administrators, and strengthen both schools on the same campus. Ultimately the LAUSD administrators and board members agreed to the arrangement. Synergy now shares expenses, such as maintenance and operations, school police, and property insurance.[44]
- The Philadelphia School Partnership (PSP), launched in 2010 by a private investor, was created to accelerate the pace of positive school options in the

city. PSP raises philanthropic funds and invests those funds to increase the number of high-quality schools in Philadelphia, by fostering knowledge sharing and learning across public, parochial, charter, and independent schools, and by coordinating the effective use of school facilities.[45]

- Houston's Spring Branch district has formed a partnership with two charter management organizations—KIPP and YES Prep. KIPP (Knowledge is Power Program) will launch a middle school within an existing district school, and YES Prep will open a high school that will absorb students from two district middle schools. In addition to starting the schools, KIPP will provide leadership training and YES Prep will provide teacher training.[46]

In considering the increasing number of collaborations between the district and charter sectors, anecdotal evidence suggests that the relationship continues to evolve. Many of the first efforts at collaboration were more likely to be about administrative services and shared facilities, rather than teaching and learning, as these are largely pragmatic collaborations. In thinking about the future, as trust builds between administrators and teachers from different sectors, will collaboration focus more directly on sharing promising practices? Understanding the nature of these partnerships and the contextual conditions necessary for such work promises to be an important area of future research.

———— ■■■ ————

CHAPTER EIGHT

What Unintended Consequences
Have Been Brought About
by Charter Schools?

THIS CHAPTER IS DIFFERENT from the others in this volume, explor-
ing not the goals but rather the unintended consequences, both negative and positive, of the charter school movement; that is, those
consequences that were not planned for and not part of the legislative intent. In Vergari's edited volume profiling the political tales
of how charter laws came to be, the chapter authors almost always
mention the same two warnings that charter opponents used to
voice their concerns: charter schools will lead to resegregated
schools and to student sorting by performance (e.g., "cream-skim-
ming" or "cherry-picking").[1] So although these potential outcomes
cannot be called unanticipated, they certainly were not included as
goals in state charter school laws.

Similarly, charter school laws were written with the intention
that founders would create and operate new or converted schools,
but no mention was made in the original laws of the potential
for networks of charter schools to emerge. The two laws that do
mention replication as a goal, Virginia's 1998 law and Massachusetts's 1993 law, speak in terms of a goal of replicating charter

school models in other public schools. The emergence of the first charter management organization (CMO) in the late 1990s and the explosion of this network approach to charter schooling is clearly another unanticipated consequence of charter schools, although whether a positive or negative consequence is perhaps up for debate.

In this chapter, we review the empirical evidence on resegregation and sorting in charter schools, and also recent studies of CMO scale-ups and their effects.

HAVE CHARTER SCHOOLS PRODUCED RESEGREGATION?

In significant flashpoints in legislative debates about charter schools, opponents have raised the argument that as schools of choice, charters would attract only one kind of student (usually defined racially or ethnically), and that this outcome would produce resegregation in the public schools. Ironically, magnet schools, the first modern version of schools of choice enacted by Congress in the 1960s, were developed explicitly to have the opposite effect; magnet schools were intended to assist districts with desegregating public schools by attracting students (regardless of where they lived in the district) to schools based on academic interests that were not associated with any particular racial or ethnic group—arts-themed magnets, math and science magnets, magnet schools that offer International Baccalaureate degrees, and so forth. Studies of magnet schools have found that for multiple reasons, including the time incurred by students to commute outside their neighborhood, magnets needed some help to accomplish their intended purpose. School districts created and enforced demographic ratios to create a racial/ethnic balance, and transportation was often provided to all students, so that the costs associated with traveling to school would not deter students from attending a magnet school. Very similar issues arose with charter schools.

Although enacted on a state-by-state basis, all charter schools are obliged by federal law to offer enrollment to any student and to hold a lottery if more students seek to enroll than spaces are available. However, some studies have pointed to the ability of charter schools to replicate inequalities through subtle forms of selection. Ausbrooks, for example, found that more than half of the thirty-six states with charter school laws at the time were "silent on the issue of geographic boundaries, and those that include provisions include no guidance as to how boundaries may be established without discriminating against certain racial and socioeconomic groups."[2] In addition, Ausbrooks found that almost half of the state laws were also silent on the issue of student transportation, creating a disadvantage for students without their own means of transportation, and nearly three-quarters were silent with regard to information dissemination, tacitly allowing the schools to market to specific neighborhoods or types of families.

These legislative silences—as well as charges that choice programs were shaped by political and economic forces of the middle and upper-middle classes to marginalize low-income and minority families—fueled allegations that charter schools led to increased segregation.[3] However, empirical findings suggest the outcomes are mixed, with different research methods and samples leading to contradictory findings.

Some studies have noted a trend of charter schools serving disproportionate numbers of minority students. This has been particularly evident for African American students, who were shown in several studies to enroll in charter schools serving high percentages of African American students.[4] One study found that African American students enrolled in charter schools with higher concentrations of African American students in five of seven locales.[5] Similarly, another study found that the average black student enrolled in a charter attended school with a higher percentage of black students and a lower percentage of white students than her non-charter counterpart.[6] A study of charter schools in North Carolina also came up with a similar conclusion: the typical African American charter school student attended a school that was more than 70 percent African American, while his counterpart in non-charter schools attended schools that were less than 50 percent African American.[7]

In contrast to the studies that found charter schools served disproportionate numbers of minority students, other research findings have concluded the opposite: charter schools served disproportionate numbers of white students.[8] Analysis of a large national database—the National Center for Education Statistics (NCES) Common Core of Data and the Schools and Staffing Survey—found that "whites who attended schools with nonwhites continue to look for options that are even more white."[9] In a small study of a charter school that was the only one in its district, the charter had the lowest percentage of both African American students and students qualifying for free and reduced-price meals compared with the other schools in the district. Similarly, in another case study, a school that converted from a regular public school to a charter school maintained a predominately white student population through activism and capitalizing on political and economic local and state connections.[10]

Segregation patterns partly depended on the region of the country in which charter schools were located, with charter schools in the West, South, and Midwest enrolling a higher percentage of white students than charter schools in the Northeast.[11] The differences may have been partly due to the fact that more nonwhite students in the Northeast attended non-charter schools, with many white students having chosen private school options. On the other hand, another study focused on Arizona, Colorado, Kansas, and North Carolina concluded that the majority of charter school students were white, with percentages similar to those in regular public schools.[12] Charter school students also were mostly white in Alaska, Hawaii, Mississippi, and Nevada, even though non-charter school students were not. In Connecticut, Illinois, Indiana, Massachusetts, Michigan, New Jersey, New York, Ohio, Pennsylvania, and Wisconsin, the majority of charter students were minority, while regular public school students were not.

Different segregation patterns also were seen along lines other than racial/ethnic. Garcia, for example, found increased segregation at the elementary level but not in high schools in Arizona.[13] In addition, segregation was related to level of parent education;

charter schools in North Carolina served a higher percentage of students whose parents have four-year college degrees.[14] In another, smaller study of a large urban district in Florida, charter school enrollment appeared to be influenced by gender; some charter schools had higher enrollments of females.[15]

Other studies found little evidence of segregation in charter schools.[16] In a study of integration in eight charter states, the racial composition of the charter schools entered by transferring students was similar to that of the non-charter schools from which the students came, with exceptions in Philadelphia and in Texas, where transfers to charter schools marginally reduced integration, and in Chicago, where charter schools marginally increased racial integration.[17] Similarly, an analysis of student demographics in 3,874 elementary school attendance zones in the nation's twenty-two largest school districts concluded that while the existence of private schools correlated strongly with reduced percentages of whites in neighborhood schools, the presence of specialty, charter, and magnet schools had a weak association with segregation in non-charter public schools.[18]

WHAT FACTORS CONTRIBUTE TO RESEGREGATION IN CHARTER SCHOOLS WHERE IT EXISTS?

Some researchers have focused on answering the question of what causes increased segregation in charter schools where it does exist. In a review of the research, it was found that many choice programs were designed to provide education to selective student populations, such as gifted or special-needs students, and that charter schools focusing on gifted education disproportionately served white students.[19] Similarly, Garcia found that at-risk, traditional, and Montessori charter schools in Arizona were more integrated than non-charter schools, while college preparatory and back-to-basics charter schools were more racially segregated than non-charters.[20]

Even though bound by open enrollment laws, studies have found that school choice programs formally and informally allowed schools to select students. In a small-scale study, the charter school maintained low integration through the use of parent contracts, and "a strict discipline code that was reported by several people interviewed to effectively exit 'unruly' students."[21] A qualitative study of eight charter schools in seven states found that recruitment strategies served to circumvent open enrollment laws by focusing publicity on reaching the desired student population by canvassing targeted neighborhoods or posting fliers at select community centers.[22]

Parent preference was linked with charter school segregation in multiple studies.[23] Rather than encouraging integration, these studies found that when given a choice, many parents choose to send their children to schools with children and families from the same race.[24] Lack of integration is also attributed to the finding that parents from different demographic groups select schools for different reasons, resulting in homogeneous student groupings based on preference for what the school offers. For example, a survey of 1,006 parents in Texas found that "28 percent of whites cited test scores as being the most important concern, while 33.9 percent of blacks said their most important concern was for the teaching of moral values . . . while for Hispanic parents good discipline is the primary consideration."[25]

Although some self-segregation in charter schools was due to parent preference, school type also played a role in segregating charter school students.[26] New-start charter schools were more segregated than conversions, according to NCES data from the Schools and Staffing Survey and Common Core of Data. Similarly, the more segregated a district was to begin with, the higher the percent of charter school students who were African American.

Other findings suggest students will be drawn to a specific charter school because of its mission, irrespective of the extent to which it is segregated. Of African American charter school students in North Carolina who made racially segregating transfers, 34.2 percent transferred into a charter school that, according to its mission statement, explicitly targeted at-risk students.[27] In some cases, serving at-risk students was the main goal of the charter school, not integration, leading founders to establish charter schools in neighborhoods with large numbers of the students they wanted to target.[28] Unfortunately, there is some evidence that strategic placement of charter schools was used to accomplish less than righteous goals. A study of New Jersey charter schools concluded that the schools tended to "position themselves along district lines to minimize enrollments by students in their host district and maximize enrollments by students in adjacent school districts who may be deemed more desirable."[29]

Similar to the relationship between school mission and student population, a 2008 review of research studies argued that "certain charters segregate by student achievement or disability because they are designed to meet differing academic needs of specific student populations. They serve students along the achievement and ability continuum: special education students, adjudicated youth, English language learners, teen parents, and gifted and talented students."[30] With regard to special education, in particular, one study found that charter schools that targeted special education students positively affected white enrollment. The hypothesis offered by the study authors speculated that "parents of white special needs students may be especially likely to send their children to charter schools because special education classrooms in [non-charter public] schools tend to have higher proportions of nonwhites than the schools in which they are located."[31]

While school type may have an impact on segregation, a large-scale study of forty-one state charter statutes found that "the state statutory language on student body population did not seem to have an impact on the integration of the student body of the schools."[32] Schools in states with provisions around racial integration, for example, were still bound by law to use blind lotteries for student admissions. On the flip side, in case studies of eight charter schools, principals reported that racial diversity requirements (and lotteries, in some cases) were not monitored or enforced and therefore not enacted. The principals of the study schools, who had all previously been teachers in low performing, high-poverty non-charter schools, relied more heavily on the local school district than on state laws for guidance in navigating legal matters related to recruitment and admissions.[33] Another problem cited in a case study of a large urban district in Florida pointed out that legislation in Florida requiring charter schools to have student enrollments that are "representative of their community" was vague, as "community" can be interpreted to mean different things (e.g., a neighborhood or the whole district).[34]

In contrast to these conclusions suggesting that state legislation has little effect on the racial composition of charter schools, another set of studies concluded the opposite. Using the 1999–2000 Schools and Staffing Survey, paired with Common Core Data information and state legislation, researchers in their analysis of 870 charter schools concluded that state legislation was an important factor in increasing African American enrollment.[35] Another large-scale review of thirty-two statutes concluded that statutory language requiring charter schools to comply with desegregation decrees and to promote diversity had the greatest impact in reducing segregation.[36] In fact, state charter school laws with a specific race proviso that required charter schools to comply with or reach district demographic averages had a statistically significant 5.03 percent higher African American enrollment.[37] Another interaction between state laws and segregation was seen in the fact that some state laws (e.g., Missouri and Indiana) restrict charter schools to urban areas, which have higher minority populations than the state as a whole.[38]

Although the bulk of the research found greater segregation in charter schools than in other public schools, the effects on the greater system have been shown to be limited. One study suggested, "Because there are relatively few charters in most school districts, it is unlikely that they affect the racial composition of the other schools in the host district."[39] Similarly, an examination of student enrollment at fifty-nine charter schools in 3,780 elementary school attendance boundaries in twenty-one of the largest U.S. school districts found that "the presence of magnet and charter schools in a catchment area has a negligible effect on the poverty rates of neighborhood schools."[40]

In sum, the evidence suggests that charter schools generally are not intentionally seeking to resegregate the public school system. But, by that same token, we find little evidence that charter schools are systematically reducing students' isolation by race or ability.

ARE CHARTER SCHOOLS ATTRACTING AN OVERABUNDANCE OF THE "CRÈME DE LA CRÈME" STUDENTS FROM NON-CHARTER PUBLIC SCHOOLS?

In addition to the worry that charter schools would result in more highly segregated schools, some predicted that charter schools would "cherry-pick" or "cream-skim" the highest performing students away from non-charter public schools. A review of early research on charter schools found that "how a school advertises and what requirements it imposes (e.g., a parent involvement contract) may narrow the range of students who seek admission."[41] Carrying out "nondiscriminatory" policies in a "discriminatory" manner was also the theme of a study of three California charter middle schools which found that financial challenges led one of the charter schools, located in a low-income area, to filter out the lowest performing students through a variety of preenrollment procedures that included complicated application processes, the use of parent contracts, and discouraging parents about the school's ability to provide special education services. In a similar vein, another early study of 30 charter schools and 147 non-charters in the District of Columbia found that so-called market-driven charter schools served fewer disadvantaged students not by "skimming" but by what the authors termed "cropping," that is, by not offering special services for Title I students, English language learners, or special education students.[42]

In contrast, later in the movement, by 2008, a review of seven studies that evaluated the effectiveness of KIPP (Knowledge is Power Program) charter schools found no strong evidence of a selective admissions process.[43] In another study, published in 2009, the authors found no evidence that charter school lotteries in New York City were not completely random.[44]

Important to recognize is the development of authorizer practices over the evolution of the charter school movement. Whereas in the early years of charter schools authorizers had little guidance in how to conduct their work, by 2004 the National Association of Charter School Authorizers (NACSA) had developed principles and standards for quality authorizing, which emphasized strong oversight to deter and, eventually, eliminate charter schools whose practices were discriminatory. NACSA's efforts may be fruitful: a 2009 study found that students entering charter schools had slightly higher test scores than their peers in the schools they left in two of seven locations studied, and their scores were identical to or lower than those of their non-charter peers in the other five locations.[45] Overall, the evidence from this study suggests that charter schools were not skimming high-achieving students. Further, transfers had surprisingly little effect on racial distribution across the sites; typically, students transferring to charter schools moved to schools with similar racial distributions as the schools from which the students came. In sum, although some studies find evidence of increased segregation and skimming, the practices are not widespread or systematic.[46]

THE UNINTENDED CONSEQUENCE OF CHARTER SCHOOL NETWORKS

Over the years, the one-by-one approach to charter schools was joined by the growth of networks of charter schools in order to spur the speed of systemic reform. First, for-profit education management organizations (EMOs) joined the educational landscape, designed to provide educational services to schools in a manner that leverages economies of scale to yield fiscal profits. EMOs, which are for-profit companies, were not originally envisioned as part of the charter school movement but rather were first developed to manage non-charter public schools. As the charter school sector developed, EMOs were well positioned to enter the market. According to the research, EMOs have varied in scale, size, and geographic spread; in educational design; in the level of prescription of the model; in use of external/internal incentives; and in targeted (e.g., at-risk) student populations.[47] Some of the EMOs profiled in the past decade of charter school research have included Edison Schools Inc., National Heritage Academies, Chancellor Beacon Academies, Mosaica Education, and SABIS.[48]

EMOs were more recently joined by their nonprofit counterparts, charter management organizations (CMOs). A CMO is a nonprofit organization that manages multiple charter schools with a common mission and instructional design and with a home office management team that offers ongoing support to its schools. According to the National Alliance for Public Charter Schools, in the 2009–2010 school year there were 637 EMO-affiliated charter schools along with 775 schools affiliated with CMOs. Together, they educated 34.6 percent of all students attending charters nationwide. As shown in figure 8.1, CMOs and EMOs are heavily concentrated in certain states.

The explosion in the growth of charter networks may be in response to several trends in the educational environment. First, individual charter schools have not had the rapid, large-scale, systemic impact originally intended by charter reformers. Studies on student performance in charter schools have shown mixed results (see chapter 3), and the intended innovation in educational instructional design—a stated goal of many state charter laws—may not be occurring to the extent expected (see chapter 2).[49]

The network approach has also grown in direct response to the operational and financial challenges faced by many stand-alone charter schools. Specifically, individual charter schools have most frequently closed because of financial and governance mismanagement issues.[50] Network configurations may combat the pervasive resource scarcity experienced by stand-alone charter schools by seeking to take advantage of economies of scale as service providers and to provide opportunities for collaboration across schools. For instance, the CMO home office offers schools specific expertise in key organizational areas, such as financial management, facility acquisition, legal compliance, grants management, and human resources. By concentrating these responsibilities in

FIGURE 8.1
EMOs/CMOs by state (2010)

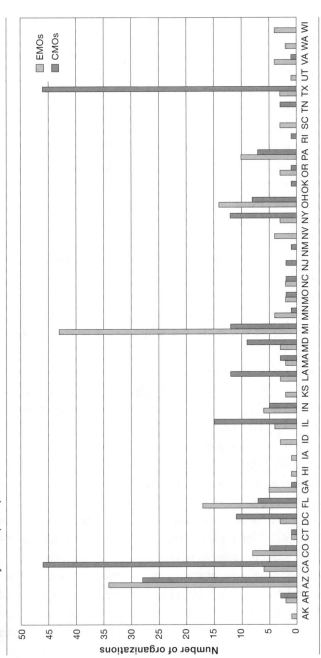

Source: Miron et al., "Profiles of For-Profit and Nonprofit Education Management Organizations" (Boulder, CO: National Education Policy Center, 2012).

Note: In "Profiles of For-Profit and Nonprofit Education Management Organizations," Miron distinguishes management organizations as for-profit and nonprofit EMOs. In this graph, we refer to these as EMOs and CMOs, respectively.

a centralized management team, in theory, principals and school leaders are able to focus on their responsibilities as instructional leaders at the school site. A network of schools, compared to individual charters, may also be able to access economies of scale in purchasing supplies and equipment and in sharing staff positions across schools.

As for CMOs, much of their growth has been attributed to the infusion of foundation funding, estimated at over half a billion dollars by 2009.[51] For instance, San Francisco–based NewSchools Venture Fund (NSVF) invests almost exclusively in CMOs, and in March 2009 the Bill and Melinda Gates Foundation announced their new $18.5 million School Networks Initiative to support the work of CMOs.[52] These and other venture philanthropies support CMO growth through funding school start-up costs, long-term capacity-building efforts, operations, home office support, and facilities.[53] They also indirectly support the growth of CMOs through investment in charter support organizations, state and national charter advocacy groups, research organizations, and other reform-minded education organizations such as Teach for America or New Leaders for New Schools.

The rapid increase in network-affiliated charter schools has given rise to research that examines the performance of CMOs relative to stand-alone charter schools. Interestingly, a national study of CMO performance concluded that the achievement impacts for CMOs are more positive than negative, at least at the middle school level: "The number of CMOs with significant positive middle school impacts is larger than the number with significant negative impacts."[54] The conclusions from this report further suggest that some CMOs are systematically outperforming others. According to the report, most of the variation in school-level impacts occurs *between* CMOs rather than within CMOs. Similarly, another study found that California charters run by management organizations scored significantly higher than other charter schools, after controlling for differences in enrollment and student characteristics.[55]

QUESTIONS FOR THE FUTURE

———•———

The research assessing the unintended (but in some cases not unanticipated) consequences of charter schools relating to resegregation and skimming points to some instances of each, but not to widespread cases of either. Recently, two reports looked at "integrated-by-design" schools—schools that have racial and socioeconomic diversity as part of their school mission.[56] In a National Association of Public Charter Schools (NAPCS) report, the lead author argued that "integrated schools seem to be designed to solve a concrete problem in a very specific neighborhood or city."[57] The report also noted that "the past decade or so . . . has seen a noteworthy rise in high-performing public charter schools with missions intentionally designed to serve racially and economically integrated student populations."[58] Future research should examine the prevalence of these integrated-by-design schools, since knowledge of them is currently limited to anecdotal evidence from the national charter advocacy group.

The perhaps more unexpected consequence not anticipated at the onset of charter schools is that charter school networks have emerged as an integral part of today's charter school landscape. As a fairly new phenomenon, there are several unanswered questions relating to CMOs. If the academic success identified in early studies of CMO performance is supported by additional research, these questions arise: What is unique about these models, in terms of their organizational structure or education program? Why are they successful, and can these innovations be adapted to the district settings?

On the other hand, as CMOs continue to scale up, are they in danger of replicating the bureaucratic structures associated with traditional school districts if their networks become too large? In other words, could too much scale-up be a bad thing? Further, given the financial, human capital, and real estate requirements for growing these networks, how sustainable are CMOs as a long-term solution?

From a policy perspective, questions remain about the relationship between authorizers and CMOs: Should authorizers treat CMOs differently in their chartering applications, oversight, or renewal procedures if the CMO has a track record of strong performance? Should there be a "fast-pass" for successful CMOs? Given the variety of charter authorizing policies, what might be done to assist CMOs to replicate successful models across state lines? Should the federal government, for example, step in to encourage the growth of CMO-affiliated charter schools in multiple states? Finally, state charter legislation was originally crafted with the single-site charter school model in mind. With the addition of CMOs in the chartering sector, to what extent should state legislation be amended? Is there a role for federal, state, and local policies in facilitating and regulating the scale-up of high-quality CMOs?

CHAPTER NINE

--- ■■■ ---

Reflections and Commentary

MORE THAN TWENTY YEARS AGO in Minnesota, a Democratic state senator with support from a Republican governor launched a movement that promised to fundamentally restructure who governs and operates public schools in the United States. Some observers thought charter schools would be a fringe movement that would stay in quirky Minnesota, the only state with the Democratic-Farmer-Labor Party. But that was not the case. As of this writing, forty-one states and the District of Columbia have voted in charter schools, and over time they have become a part of the national education discourse. Will the movement continue to grow in the future? Will it become the dominant mode of operation? Or will the movement be trivialized over time? During one of the interviews that form the basis for this chapter, Paul Hill, a longtime school reformer, predicted: "I don't think the charter school movement is going to be something people look back on and say, 'Cluck-cluck, we did this, and now we don't anymore.'"

We have organized this book according to the range of stated purposes—as proclaimed in state laws—behind the adoption of charter school laws. The individual chapters have examined the empirical research in order to shed light on the evidence as it pertains to these legislated purposes, answering the question of whether the research results show that the goals were met, were not met, or, as in most cases, were mixed based on study contexts and methods. We grounded the chapters within three specific domains: classrooms, schools, and the broader public education system. Our hope is that this volume will serve as a gateway to the next generation of policy makers, educators, and researchers in all three domains and across the spectrum of charter school proponents, skeptics, and agnostics.

As mentioned in the Introduction, we have made an effort to explore crosscutting themes in order to assess new directions for charter school policy and practice. To introduce a broad view, we posed four overarching questions. In this final chapter, we return to the questions first presented at the beginning of the book:

- In what ways, if any, have charter schools challenged the definition and boundaries of public education?
- Across the levels of the system—classroom, school, district— where have charters succeeded? Where have they fallen short?
- How is the relationship between charter and non-charter public schools changing? How is the role of charters in the education sector as a whole evolving?
- Most policies last ten to twenty years before being eclipsed by "the next big thing." What does the charter sector have to do in the next five years to assure its future?

To enhance the breadth and depth of our conversation about charter schools—looking back and moving forward—we asked five informed researchers and reformers to join our conversation. Together they represent a variety of perspectives, from enthusiasts to skeptics, on the accomplishments and shortcomings of charter schools and the charter school movement.

One of the commentators on the enthusiastic end of the continuum is Dr. Bruno V. Manno. Manno, along with Chester E. Finn Jr. and Gregg Vanourek, wrote one of the first books on charters,

Charter Schools in Action (2001), which offered an early look at how charter schools were emerging in the first states that enacted laws and at the role of charters schools "in renewing American public education itself."[1] Another enthusiast we interviewed is Dr. Deborah McGriff, who has deep roots in traditional school districts. McGriff's work is now with NewSchools Venture Fund, where she leads the National Network of Charter Schools. The third commentator in this part of the spectrum is Dr. Paul T. Hill, founder of the Center on Reinventing Public Education. Hill opened the center in 1993 and has a long history of being the "father of invention," creating new ideas about how the U.S. public education systems can be restructured.

In the realm of skeptics, we have included a moderate skeptic and a full-blown skeptic. Our moderate skeptic is Dr. Jeffrey R. Henig, a professor of political science at Columbia University and a professor of political science and education at Columbia University's Teachers College. Our final contributor is Dr. Charles M. Payne, the Frank P. Hixon Distinguished Service Professor in the School of Social Service Administration at the University of Chicago, where he is also affiliated with the Urban Education Institute. He noted in his interview that he has "moved from neutral to increasingly skeptical." Although these characterizations of our commentators are useful to help frame their perspectives, it is important to note that they each exhibit shades of enthusiasm and skepticism. Their views are not as clearly aligned as the characterization of pros versus cons suggests. Rather, one group could be characterized as roughly but far from uniformly on the positive side, and the other as roughly but far from uniformly on the negative side.

We interviewed each of the five commentators individually and used our four overarching questions to guide the conversations. We taped the interviews, which lasted about forty-five minutes to an hour. In this chapter, we examine the range of reflections offered by these commentators about the results of charter schools thus far and seek to bring them together with a clear focus on moving forward.

QUESTION 1: IN WHAT WAYS, IF ANY, HAVE CHARTER SCHOOLS CHALLENGED THE DEFINITION AND BOUNDARIES OF PUBLIC EDUCATION?

In reviewing the findings from chapters 1–8, one big takeaway is that charter schools have opened up what we think of as public education, but the movement has not totally revolutionized it—it's a matter of degree. Charter schools have pushed the public education system toward new approaches to school governance, new roles for teachers, parents, and public-private partnerships, and new ways of replicating or scaling up successful schools. But the essence of what makes a school a school has not been altered—at least not in any widespread way—by the introduction of charter schools into the education sphere.

In our conversations about how charters have expanded the definition and boundaries of public education, several commentators' thoughts echoed the most prevalent legislative purposes behind charter schools. Manno referred to the twin goals of increased autonomy (chapter 4) and increased accountability (chapter 6)—found in fourteen and twenty-seven state laws, respectively—in stating that "charters do push the envelope in the ways we think about school autonomy and accountability. When charters started they were subject to very specific performance contracts that were part of the charter. This is something that was an innovation; not to say there weren't schools that existed that had performance contracts, but these were not thought of as ordinary schools." Payne emphasized the goal to increase options for all families, one of the specific goals we included under the broad heading of increased competition (chapter 7). As he put it, "It's not that charters are necessarily doing something different or that families have a commitment to charters, per se. It may just be that families are desperate for alternatives. People are looking for something that is better—safer environments where their children are going to get a higher level of instruction." Hill's thoughts were in line with the goal of providing new options for teachers (chapter 1): "There is the idea that teaching careers can be much more varied than was the norm before charter schools in terms of being open to people not from education schools, career changers, or practitioners from the community, like music teachers." In addition to attracting new people into the teaching profession, Manno pointed to the new opportunities provided to teachers, arguing that "charter school teachers have much more control over the learning environment, not just in classrooms, but also in developing the culture of learning in schools."

Notably, in discussing the four most prevalent legislative purposes—new opportunities for teachers, education program innovations, accountability, and competition—only one of the commentators mentioned seeing charters deliver on innovation in curriculum and instruction, a finding in line with the lack of widespread education program innovation reported on in the empirical research (see chapter 2). Alluding to this goal, Hill noted in passing that "charter schools have started to break down the boundaries of what we normally think of as the school in one place at a particular time. I'm thinking of hybrid and cyber charters."

Without much education program innovation to point to, the commentators tended instead to highlight ways in which charters had produced innovations at the school and the system levels, most notably around governance. At the school level, several commentators mentioned the recent phenomenon of charters replicating through the scale-up of charter management organizations. "The move to scale from one site to CMOs provided a new governance arrangement, with a focus on quality and reputation . . . There isn't much attention to replicating the most successful schools in districts, but replicating high performing schools is something that's been encouraged by charters," said McGriff, adding, "I don't think that the current portfolio approach to charters or charter districts, or district-charter partnerships, would have been pursued without the growth of charter schools."

As mentioned in chapter 2, the empirical research reviewed for this book includes studies of the prevalence of partnerships to manage charter schools and to deliver education services. Hill noted the use of partnerships among New York City charters "that are aligned with businesses, getting kids into internships. This was not unheard of before, but it is clearer that these parties can now participate more than before chartering came around. Charter schools have helped to integrate and break down barriers." Manno extended this notion by suggesting a demand-driven approach of different charter schools partnering to provide services that cater to the specific needs of different families:

> Consider a low-income family where there is a single mother and three kids with very few social networks. That kind of environment makes it tough when the mother needs to make a school choice that matches her child. That situation is different from someone who is still lower-middle class, still a single mom but has access to some social networks (e.g., church, intergenerational support), which is different from a two-parent family with both parents working. We need different kinds of ways to think about segmenting services to these different kinds of families who may need different intermediary organizations. We need to get more sophisticated at segmenting families and students, and creating organizations that can work with these different needs and match them to the appropriate kind of environments and learning technologies that are needed.

At the system level, charters were credited with an important innovation in governance: shaking up teacher unions and school districts from engaging in "business as usual." As Payne noted based on observations of public schools nationwide, "The great thing about the charter movement is that it has made unions change. Unions are afraid of charters, so they are getting their act together. Fear of the charters has moved the unions in a much healthier direction. In Chicago, unions are now talking about putting into place thinner contracts. They are talking about educational issues, reviving a discussion about education issues inside schools, and this is out of respect for the charters." Similarly, Hill noted the move of school districts toward new governance arrangements as a reaction to charters. Thus far, several dozen school districts have begun to restructure their school systems through portfolio management approaches and district redesign as a tool for improving all district schools. Hill explained the approach:

> The school district uses the term "portfolio" to say they are developing options: inviting new people into the district, offering new ways of educating new teachers, and holding all schools to the same performance standards. As I see it, the core theory of action of the portfolio approach is that you increasingly create autonomy for regular schools, keep working on them until all schools can be autonomous. The idea that you can attract principals who want to operate differently, and teachers who want to work differently, and districts that want to use money differently, is attractive to a lot of district people.

While the commentators mostly mentioned specific innovations that charters had pushed into the mainstream of public education, Henig had a different take. "The result," he said, "is not necessarily greater diversity in the range of schools available to families. Rather, charters have been a vehicle for more quickly instituting change."

QUESTION 2: ACROSS THE LEVELS OF THE SYSTEM—CLASSROOM, SCHOOL, DISTRICT—WHERE HAVE CHARTERS SUCCEEDED? WHERE HAVE THEY FALLEN SHORT?

In assessing the successes and pitfalls of charter schools and the movement, the commentators discussed the effects in charter classrooms and schools, addressing such topics as whether charters have fostered high levels of parent engagement and whether they have resulted in increased student integration or segregation. And, of course, they tackled the issue of student achievement.

As noted in the Introduction, increasing parent engagement was one of the commonly included purposes mentioned in state charter school laws. Charter schools were created as schools of choice, and as such, parents are involved from day one by making the choice to enroll their child. The notion from the research literature connecting parent involvement to higher student performance also appears to have influenced charter developers. McGriff hit on the point directly: "Charters would not exist if they could not convince parents to enroll their children. When kids have to apply to get in, when you're an open enrollment school, you won't exist [based on] zoning policies [that allocate students automatically to district-run public schools]. Charters have been able to attract parents, and many have long waiting lists. Charter schools have been successful at empowering parents."

Manno, on the other hand, challenged the value of parent choice regulating the market: "The lines are getting blurrier and blurrier over who is doing what and who is acting in response to what. The environment is becoming more like a social market—a public market with few regulations. But it is naïve to think there will be no regulations. Some people argue that parent choice alone should regulate the market, but I don't think that is going to happen." Henig was more skeptical and questioned how much we really know about parent engagement: "The research on parent engagement is thin and doesn't offer a meaningful understanding of the parent side of things. What does parent engagement mean, does it make a difference? Do charters facilitate more parent engagement of the good kind than not?"

On the topic of integration versus segregation, Henig observed that charters had fallen short in contributing to a more integrated public school system:

> There were folks out there who said the choice model would lead to a more natural and sustainable integration at the school level. The source of *de facto* segregation was residential patterns, and decoupling schools from neighborhoods would lead to re-sorting student populations by interest. That would lead to integrated schools, but I don't think that the evidence supports that vision. And, for good reason it didn't happen. The concern that opponents had early on was that there would be great dramatic emphasis, on the part of

charters, to cream and look for constituencies that were less disadvantaged. Instead, charters made an effort to target where the need was greatest, that was in cities with a dominance of blacks or Latinos. Given where the charter schools are located and the demand, they ended up being predominantly black or Latino. Early on, proponents suggested that there would be a natural integration because of choice. But that didn't happen.

By contrast, McGriff did not view the key mission of charter schools as educating underserved students. Instead, she argued that a principal purpose of the charter movement was to provide additional educational options to parents, one of the purposes charter laws stressed also. She continued, "A few states have policies that target specific groups of students—at-risk students, for example. But after twenty years, families are enrolling in charters because they want something different from what their traditional public school offers, and they can get it through a charter school."

McGriff's main concern about the lack of diversity in the charter movement stressed charter school leadership, both at the board and school levels:

In order to survive the next big thing in education, charter schools will need to pay attention to the lack of diversity in terms of school leadership. The charter school board is responsible for the school's success. We need diversity on charter boards and among the founders of charters. I don't think the diversity of charter communities is represented at any level of the system. Some organizations are developing leadership programs to encourage racial diversity among charter leaders. For the movement to continue to educate underserved kids, there needs to be more sensitivity to the diversity of charter school leaders. Some charter operators are recruiting college graduates from their alumni base to develop diverse groups of teachers and leaders. We started this movement without sensitivity, and hopefully in the next twenty years, we'll be more sensitive to the issue of leadership diversity.

Finally, student outcomes were hotly contested, with commentators mixed along "party lines"; supporters noted positive outcomes, detractors highlighted performance shortcomings. On the success side of the debate, McGriff noted the focus of some charters on preparing low-income students for college. This aim is evident in school mission statements where the curriculum is discussed as "college prep." Many of these schools, both independent and connected to charter management organizations, judge their success in terms of students' acceptance into college. In taking stock of their success, McGriff traced the evolution of the college prep public charters:

> When the charter movement began, most charters had a goal of outperforming comparable schools. Then they wanted to outperform district schools. Then the goal was helping low-income kids do better. When there was evidence of that, the discussion turned to college enrollment. Today, the highest performing charter schools are talking about college readiness: Low-income kids are going to be ready for college. That's the most powerful contribution of the movement. When underserved kids attend and complete college, you increase by 50 percent the likelihood that their kids won't be in poverty. It's all about transforming communities—providing equity for the underserved.

The skeptics among the commentators offered up several important points about the areas in which charters have fallen short of expectations. Henig pointed directly to the impact of charters on student achievement:

> Charter schools haven't had the impact on test scores (which was their measure of choice) that proponents initially trumpeted as possible and I think believed would come about. A lot of the proponents genuinely believed that the reason test scores were flat and unimpressive in international comparisons was because people at the school level were not trying hard. One of the things they learned was that even when they tried hard and did smart things, it didn't lead to sharp increases in test scores. I think there was naïveté at the

extreme, especially on the part of funders, but not the people in the field. The funders believed that public sector monopolies put adult interests above children's interests—people who saw poverty as a reason not to work hard. They were surprised to find the challenges were more substantial than they expected.

Payne was similarly disturbed by the low performance of charters, and he posited the idea that charters were consuming resources that could have been invested in reforms with bigger payoffs:

From the data I know, charters are probably somewhat worse than traditional publics on average. Maybe you can make a case they are slightly better. I've never seen the case that charters are a whole lot better than traditional public schools after taking the outliers out. So we should talk about other reforms—things that have a much bigger pop (early child education, for example). The charter discussion has sucked all the air out of the national discussion about how to improve student learning. The amount of time we are spending discussing charter schools, I just don't see the rationale in terms of children's outcomes.

A second area of concern relates to access to charters. Henig pointed out that there are significant gaps geographically where charters are not available: "Charters have been concentrated in a small number of places—they don't go everywhere in large numbers. Right now there's not much impetus to expand more broadly. Partly because the CMOs don't want to go to places where per-pupil funding isn't high enough, where buildings/facilities are difficult. Foundations don't want to put money into Camden, New Jersey, or Schenectady, New York. Things have been concentrated in a number of places." Payne came to a similar conclusion but through a different line of argument. Referring to Chicago, he notes that the city "has a history of putting charters into communities without consultation." He went on to say that the effect of this is a "divestment in neighborhood schools and an investment in charters, despite mediocre performance in Chicago."

QUESTION 3: HOW IS THE RELATIONSHIP BETWEEN CHARTER AND NON-CHARTER PUBLIC SCHOOLS CHANGING? HOW IS THE ROLE OF CHARTERS IN THE EDUCATION SECTOR AS A WHOLE EVOLVING?

One of the big surprises of the charter movement was that despite proponents' interests in having charter schools experiment with ways to improve schooling and student performance, school districts by and large were very resistant, and the "charter wars" ensued. "We're competitors and not collaborators" was a popular refrain, closely followed by "charters do not hold a monopoly on innovation or promising practices; non-charter publics have good ideas too." These unfriendly relationships continue to persist today in school districts; however, district-charter collaborations are on the rise.[2] Collaborations that twenty years ago would have seemed like "sacrilege and blasphemy" are now accepted.[3] Henig explained the shift toward an integrated educational system: "In some places like Chicago, Philadelphia, and others, charter schools have been integrated into a system-wide approach. It's not simply individual charter school operators bubbling up and finding a distinct niche." McGriff agreed and also stressed the need for a systemic approach:

I believe we're going to see more traditional school districts embrace charters as part of their reform initiative. The high performing charters that want to scale aren't going to a new city for one school. For high performing charters, districts will have to make commitments for multiple sites and agree to open, say, five schools, based on the quality and success of their other schools. This is already happening in Memphis and Milwaukee. Unless you offer a CMO the ability to build a substantial network, they won't be able to establish the concentration of schools needed to provide the support and to attract the talent. Another reason behind the changing relationship between district and charters is the Gates district-charter contract cities, where synchronicity is being promoted. Charters, especially CMOs which have the political clout, are going to be more assertive at the federal and state levels around the policies they need to be successful.

Hill was more skeptical in his assessment: "I really do think the relationship between charters and non-charter public schools is changing. I know some charter people are concerned that the insurgent movement is causing competition that ultimately will devalue the use of the charter mechanism." He went on to express his own opinion about how the role of charters in the education sector as a whole is evolving: "I think the answer depends on how you want to look at the charter-non-charter situation. Is the charter movement being co-opted by conventional public education, or is it taking over the public education sector? New Orleans, Chicago, and Cleveland are all moving rapidly. Cleveland built some good charter-ish in-district schools, but when there was an employment cutback, the schools were wiped out, and the mayor went on the warpath."

Payne was very clear about who is co-opting whom. From his perspective, the power elite favors charter schools and this, in turn, creates acrimony between charters and other public schools. He argued, "Here in Chicago there are a group of high-flying charters that are well connected. So, while the union is against charters, the city just announced they are going to open fifty new charter schools. The charter schools also have better facilities, and more programs and equipment—they just look better than traditional schools. There is an undercurrent in the public discourse that Chicago bends over backwards to make charters look better and that a wide range have access to outside funding."

With this scenario of the haves and have-nots, Payne also brought up the role of politics in preserving the status quo: "Whether the tension between charters and non-charters will continue depends on Chicago politics and, in particular, who the next mayor will be. Charters have a lot of friends in high places, and they have an enormous advantage, in part because there is so much money behind public relations. In order to even the playing field, the research on charters will have to get awfully negative. At this point, charters are driving out discussions of substance, everywhere."

QUESTION 4: MOST POLICIES LAST TEN TO TWENTY YEARS BEFORE BEING ECLIPSED BY "THE NEXT BIG THING." WHAT DOES THE CHARTER SECTOR HAVE TO DO IN THE NEXT FIVE YEARS TO ASSURE ITS FUTURE?

Though charter schools have become an integral part of the education landscape, with well-established support at the federal level and in many states, proponents and detractors alike agree that their goal of serving as a significant vehicle for school improvement and reform has yet to be fully realized. If charter schools are to persist and thrive in an era of increasing accountability, they can no longer ride largely on their potential, but rather will need to deliver more consistently on their performance.

In conversations with the commentators, nearly all mentioned the importance of quality authorizing to the future of the charter school movement. Most charter authorizers (i.e., school districts) were drafted into the job, in contrast to charter founders, who entered the movement voluntarily, and there has been ambiguity about the authorizer role: were they to be "sponsors," as termed in Minnesota, or simply "authorizers" of charters? Was the authorizing role in addition to usual district responsibilities and, if so, would authorizers acquire extra staff and funding to assist in carrying out their new responsibilities? Were authorizers supposed to conduct routine site visits to charter schools, or was that considered micromanaging? Henig summed up the confusion around the authorizer role, saying, "The movement launched quickly and authorizers just didn't know what they were doing."

Manno reflected on the early years of the movement when authorizers were almost invisible: "Go back to *Charter Schools in Action*, there is little in there about authorizers.[4] In fact if you look in the index, 'authorizer' isn't there. I guess folks just assumed back then that this was an easy thing to do, or it was taken for granted that people would authorize only quality entities or that it would be easy to close down a school. Not a lot of thought was initially given to charter authorizing." Henig, in turn, linked the minimal authorizer role to interest group politics: "Thinking about the earlier years of the charter movement, the Center for Education Reform in Washington, DC, was the chief advocate for charter schools. Its whole message was: make it easy for charters to be authorized and have a light regulatory hand."

Regarding charter authorizing in more recent years, Manno summed up the progress this way: "We have a far better sense of the responsibilities of authorizers: the due diligence process, how to think about closing a school, and how to think about monitoring a school. We have developed a perspective on what a good authorizer does. There are still non-quality authorizers, but we have come to understand the authorizing process far better." Henig was not quite so sanguine. One of his chief concerns was the lack of data to guide charter authorizing practices: "Even now, I don't think we have sophisticated analyses at the authorizer level to say with confidence which are the ones that are intervening when they should, and which are the ones waiting for financial disasters of some kind. My suspicion is there's variation at the authorizer level, specifically around how much capacity is needed and do authorizers have it!"

Most of the commentators also mentioned a second issue—the authorizer's responsibility to close down low performing charters. As Manno succinctly stated, "Authorizers have not been fully responsible at closing schools down or improving them." McGriff concurred, saying, "I understand there are lots of reasons why closing a charter is not easy, but we have not been as aggressive in maintaining and establishing a level of quality for charter school performance. There was an expectation that we would not allow underperforming charter schools to operate forever, but this is not the case."

While evidence suggests that charters are becoming more integrated into the education landscape, Manno offered a call to action to the charter sector: step up involvement in the nation's push to help turn around chronically low performing schools. McGriff, drawing on her investment knowledge, argued that by involving charters in the turnaround business,

Reformers will get faster and more sustained improvement from the restart or turnaround model than with the transformation model, which only tinkers with small pieces (e.g., replacing the principal). Charters also have an advantage with the autonomy they bring to the turnaround effort. Several cities—New Haven, Connecticut, and Indianapolis, Indiana—are building local turnaround experts using managers of successful charter schools. Successful single-site charters and CMOs have been given charters to turn around schools through redesign of the school organization. As more investors help charters or entrepreneurs move into the turnaround market and as public funds shift to support work that allows innovators to invest in redesign, the market will expand as charters position themselves to merge the turnaround work into CMOs.

The final piece of advice from the commentators about integrating into the educational landscape concerned scale-up, which if done incorrectly, might result in more hostility toward the charter movement. Most of our commentators—all but Payne—mentioned the significant increase in recent years in the number of CMO-affiliated charter schools, a trend reported on in recent research.[5] Hill warned, "We need to think hard about limiting the industrialization of charter schools through prescriptive CMOs. CMOs have led to a lot of charter schools that are really not charter schools; they have little autonomy and are being managed by CMOs that control choices and control the people. The industrialized CMOs are top down, very top down." Henig stressed the politics of the situation and came to much the same conclusion as Hill:

I see the CMOs and EMOS as more corporate than a laissez-faire or market approach to scaling up. The irony is that the larger CMOs are muscling aside both the early conservative idea of charters—focused on entrepreneurial spirit and developing new niches—and the more progressive left, community-based vision. Instead, by going to scale, the "mom and pops" on all points of the pedagogical and ideological spectrum are becoming less significant, and with that, we've lost the idea of micro-markets that early proponents of charter schools talked about. The end result is that the large-scale providers have the political clout to shape the future direction of the charter movement away from what was originally envisioned by reformers—school-based charters.

Hill went on to offer an alternative to scaling up—the idea of an incubator adapted from the business sector:

An incubator is a better approach for scaling up charter schools than an industrialized CMO. An incubator is an organization that helps a group of people who have an idea. The incubator tries to increase the probability of success by giving the idea an early trial before the group runs a school. In my mind, that's the way to generate real innovation and diversity among public schools, instead of taking one good school and trying to replicate it. When an inventive, locally owned approach is tried first at one school and then transported to other schools, the approach turns into a bunch of band-aids for other schools.

While Manno argued for scaling up charter schools, he and Payne warned about the importance of being cognizant of the community in which the charter school resides, suggesting that a single approach to education advocated by some CMOs might not be the right approach to scaling up. As Payne assessed the situation in his city, "Chicago has a history of putting charters in a community without prior consultation. Charter schools need to work with communities at a deeper level to consider and respond to the specific needs of families." Interestingly, Manno, considered to be a charter school enthusiast, came to a conclusion similar to Payne's: "One future direction would be for charters to embed themselves in a constructive way in the life of the community where they find themselves—to see themselves not exclusively as a school, but as a center for community education and outreach. It doesn't mean charters have to desert their 'brand,' but they need to be cognizant of the wider community they exist in, be responsive to its needs and to whatever message it sends out about how the school will serve the community, educate its kids, and be a member of a wider civic community." Hill's critique of charter schools stressed their variability in terms of success:

> One finding that emerges from all the literature is that charter schools need to be a partnership between government [authorizer] and the provider [of services]. If government isn't in the game, or if it doesn't pay attention, or if it is in the game but is against charters, then you don't get much. The government's reputation needs to be on the line; if they make a mess of it, they will be disgraced. Arizona charters are a great example of the government being permissive: a lot of charter schools are serving kids whose parents might not have liked the school they were in. Washington, DC, is the other extreme: when the district was chartering, it was very politicized, not quality-oriented, and this led to very bad schools. The essence of charters is not simply to take the wraps off and let a thousand flowers bloom. If government sees charters as a way to provide good schools, does due diligence, and gives a reasonable amount of support, then this will explain the differences in performance between schools. Looking back over the past twenty years, this is a big lesson from charter schools.

The diversity of opinions shared by these commentators provides a fitting complement to the diversity of findings uncovered in the research we reviewed. Their reflections, hopes, and fears about the charter sector shine a light on the complexity of the charter concept itself and on the varied manifestations of charter schools in different neighborhoods, cities, and states.

We would like to thank our commentators for their willingness to share their personal views and challenges in making sense of charters. Our own conclusions to some of these same questions follow in the final section.

CONCLUSION

———■■■———

IN THIS BOOK we have put the charter movement and charter schools under the microscope. Earlier chapters reflected on the goals, implementation strategies, and performance outcomes of charter schools by taking a deep dive into the piles of empirical research studies about charter schools. In chapter 9, the commentators offered a range of perspectives to help identify the problems and successes of charters, looking back and looking forward. We finish the volume with a look toward the future: What is on the horizon for charter school reformers? In view of the past twenty years of research on charters, what are the new avenues to explore?

WHAT IS ON THE HORIZON FOR CHARTER SCHOOLS?

The notion of restructuring public education in the United States through charter schools was ambitious and challenging. States had to first buy into the charter movement by enacting charter laws that complemented their individual state cultures. Next, districts and other charter authorizers had to figure out what the responsibility of authorizing meant, and then set up policies and practices to carry out their new responsibility. Finally, the reform would not have been as far-reaching if founders—those already within the education system and new players alike—had not acquired the knowledge and skills to create new public schools and if parents had not taken the risk of putting their children into brand-new schools that held the promise of a different educational opportunity. During most of the past twenty years, the intentions of the charter policy champions were often overshadowed by polarizing debates and controversies over the theory of action and the implementation of the charter reform in districts and states.

As mentioned in earlier chapters, as charter schools age, they have become more and more central to the education landscape. Charter schools have gained direct access to funds previously reserved for non-charter public schools at the federal and state levels. The U.S. Department of Education awarded i3 grants to several CMOs, and two consortia of charter schools received Teacher Incentive Fund grants to support new systems for evaluating and compensating teachers. Finally, in the summer of 2012, the Broad Foundation awarded its first Broad Prize for Public Charter Schools to Houston's YES Prep Public Schools to complement the Broad District Prize, created in 2002.

In looking forward, there is some evidence that charter school leaders and policy makers are taking actions that seek to broaden the range of stakeholders that can help assure the future of the charter school movement. One trend bubbling up organically from communities expands the supply of charters to suburban and rural neighborhoods. Back in 2002, a report issued by the Thomas B. Fordham Foundation, "The Approval Barrier to Suburban Charter Schools," cautioned that "if a state sets up a system for authorizing charter schools where the only authorizing body really doesn't want charter schools, there won't be many charter schools . . . Where local districts are the primary, or sole authorizers, there won't be many charter schools, particularly in the suburbs . . . where they reject practically every charter application they receive."[1] Fast-forward to the last few years, while tensions over charters in the suburbs have not subsided, the incidence of charter petitions in suburban and rural areas, as judged by media attention and recent reports, is on the rise:

- In Montgomery County, Maryland, the school board is moving toward its first charter, a Montessori elementary school, after initially rejecting it.
- Imagine Schools, a large charter school operator, has held meetings in Loudoun County, Virginia, to gauge parental interest

in charters marketed partly as an alternative to overcrowded schools.

- In Illinois, where 103 of the current 116 charter schools are in Chicago, an Evanston school board committee is considering opening the suburban district's first charter school.[2]

According to Stuit and Doan, the evidence with respect to charter schools in rural areas is even more compelling: "Nearly half of all charter schools are found outside city limits. Notably, rural charter schools are the fastest growing segment of the sector, with nearly 20 percent of all charter schools housed in rural areas."[3] In a 2012 Issue Brief by the National Alliance for Public Charter Schools entitled "Beyond City Limits: Expanding Public Charter Schools in Rural America," the authors describe case studies of rural charter schools that have created partners with local businesses, used technology to personalize learning, and customized schools to local communities:

- The Walton Rural Life Center (WRLC), founded in 2007, is one of the few public schools—charter or non-charter—to fully integrate agriculture into its curriculum. With the support of local farmers, WRLC's 135 K–5th grade students reinforce skills learned in the classroom to a variety of real world situations.
- Julian Charter School (JCS) leverages technology to provide a K–12 curriculum to students throughout San Diego, Riverside, and Orange counties, including more than 150 rural students. JCS's academic program centers on personalized virtual learning, but students are able to supplement their home-based learning by visiting one of JCS's Learning Centers, which provide classroom instruction and one-on-one tutoring.
- As a result of its declining population, Paradox Valley, Colorado, saw its local district school close in 1999, forcing students to endure nearly three-hour commutes to attend the next nearest school. In response, the local community founded the Paradox Valley Charter School that same year to not only address

logistical issues brought on by consolidation but also take a stance toward preserving its distinctive rural culture. Paradox Valley sees itself as "a place where the community and the school work together for the literacy and vitality of our rural culture."[4]

A second approach to broadening the constituency base for the charter movement involves urban charters created to offer educational choices to the young, educated, predominately white families that have begun moving into urban neighborhoods, what William Frey of the Brookings Institution calls "bright flight."[5] In this vein, Eva Moskowitz, founder of the CMO Harlem Success Academies, dropped "Harlem" in the title of her nonprofit and renamed it Success Academy Charter Schools (SACS) to attract a broader constituency. Moskowitz is now out front leading a new breed of charter management organizations that focus on serving middle- and lower-income students alike. SACS recently opened three new schools in gentrifying areas of New York City: the Upper West Side in Manhattan, and Cobble Hill and Williamsburg in Brooklyn.[6]

A final area with potential for growth is the school turnaround business. Observers predict an emergence of new charter networks that will focus specifically on turning around chronically low performing schools, as opposed to networks that already exist. Two such cases can be seen in Green Dot Public Schools and Mastery Charter Schools in Philadelphia. In these instances, both CMOs have student achievement data to back up their turnaround success. Green Dot in Los Angeles took over Locke High School in 2007 and over time transformed the campus into a series of smaller charter schools or academies. A report released in 2012 by the National Center for Research on Evaluation, Standards, and Student Testing (CRESST) at UCLA concluded that students in the Green Dot Locke academies dramatically increased their test scores and persistence in school, and also took more challenging courses than comparable peers.[7]

Mastery Charter Schools has had comparable success in most of the eight Philadelphia public schools that it has taken over, as part of the district's Renaissance program. Mastery has earned bragging rights for turning around several of the Philadelphia public schools' most violent and low performing schools. Students at Harrity, which Mastery took over in 2010, leapt seventeen points in math in one year. Last year, 55 percent of its students scored proficient or above, compared to 38 percent in 2010. Reading scores went up by ten points in 2011. Another Philadelphia public school, Shoemaker, which Mastery took over in 2006, has made steady progress as well. According to the Philadelphia Department of Education, 74 percent of Shoemaker's students scored proficient or advanced in math.

WHAT NEW AVENUES SHOULD FUTURE RESEARCH EXPLORE?

In reflecting on the research we drew from in writing these chapters, several areas in need of further research come to mind.

First, the preponderance of research on charter schools is fairly limited in scope. Quantitative measures of charter school performance are largely limited to academic performance and, as Betts and Tang commented in a recent literature review on student achievement research, "it is still the case that the majority of charter school studies take snapshots of student achievement at one point in time, or compare successive cohorts of students in a given grade."[8] Qualitative research, on the other hand, tends to be case studies of one or a few schools. Researchers have not delved much into looking inside the "black box" of schooling, or in compiling evidence-based promising practices, with the exception of the What Works Clearinghouse, an initiative out of the U.S. Department of Education's Institute of Education Sciences. There is a paucity of national studies of charter schools.

Another area for future research would be to consider how the age of a charter school affects its performance. We know from the seminal RAND Change Agent study from the 1970s and its many successors that change and implementation of policy initiatives take time.[9] This suggests some benefit to disaggregating charter schools by their age. We might expect, for example, that new charter schools (open three years or fewer) would have different goals and performance trends than emerging (open four to nine years) or mature charter schools (open ten or more years). While most past empirical research concentrates on snapshots of student achievement at one point in time, considering the age of the charter school as an explanatory variable is valuable.

In the early years, charter schools are focused on developing a mission and curriculum and recruiting staff and students. In the later years, charters often turn to creating services tailored to the particular needs of their student population. This stage, for example, often focuses on partnerships with nonprofit organizations, such as the Boys and Girls Clubs to provide after-school care, or health-oriented nonprofits that can assist charter schools with services such as eye and dental exams.

The performance effects of the length of time a student spends in a charter school also needs further investigation. After more than two decades, we now have longitudinal data where enrollment trends and graduation rates can be tracked and compared to non-charter public schools. Are students who spend their education career (K–12) at a charter school more likely to do better than students who enter a charter school at the secondary level?

In reviewing the empirical research on charter schools, we were struck by the limited measures by which charter schools were judged. Student achievement overwhelmingly was the primary dependent variable. The notion of using multiple measures—both leading and outcome indicators—to assess school performance recognizes the array of legislated goals from parent involvement to charters as autonomous organizations, as well as the charter school trajectory, from creation through to maturity. Embedded in the charter school theory of action is the idea that charters will be responsible for overseeing the finances of the school and will pay heed to the financial health of the school. However, there are few studies of financial health to balance the academic performance measures. One approach taken by the authors of California's School Performance Dashboard examines to what extent charter schools are investing their resources directly into classrooms. Other measures of performance examine the level of reserves—how much have charters saved in reserves to help them weather future costs if revenue is deficient? What is a charter school's liquidity ratio? This reflects the school's ability to pay off its short-term debts, as well as the ability to raise capital, either through selling off or borrowing against its assets. We also see value in using financial data to assess academic productivity. For example, how do charter and other public schools with similar per-pupil spending compare on academic performance?[10]

Another area for future research regarding charter school finance would be the longevity of private sector involvement. Previous research identified several unanswered questions related to charter school finance.[11] First, what motivates charter school funders to invest in charter schools and what are the implications of this for students? Will private investment continue past the development phase of charter schools? Second, the question of what private funds are being used for is critical; are private funds supplementing public funds or supplanting them? Finally, what are the effects of venture philanthropy on the charter sector, the urban education system, and the philanthropy field itself?

In addition to financial measures, charters—as schools of choice—need more precise measures of teacher, parent, and student satisfaction. Many charter schools maintain waiting lists, but there are no uniform standards. A few school districts, such as Los Angeles and New York City, require all district public schools to use satisfaction surveys as additional measures of school performance. Charter schools know community members (teachers, parents, students) are dissatisfied when they leave, but what about early detection?

Measuring "customer" satisfaction is far more prevalent with for-profit businesses; its applicability to schools of choice also seems spot-on. A pioneer in this arena is the Baldrige program, which was enacted in 1987 by an act of Congress and named after the former commerce secretary Malcolm Baldrige in the Reagan administration. In the early years, the awards targeted mainly small businesses and manufacturing companies. For about the past fifteen years, nonprofits along with government and education organizations have routinely won the Malcolm Baldrige National Quality Awards. Among the keystones for the Baldrige Award is "customer knowledge." With knowledge about customer satisfaction, organizations will be capable of delivering "an ever-improving value to customers and stakeholders," which, in turn, contributes to "organizational sustainability."[12] While some charter schools and CMOs submit "customer" satisfaction survey results as part of their renewal packages (in addition to academic performance), the idea of multiple measures—both leading and outcome indicators—which more authentically reflect the school's performance, is not considered routinely in charter school policy, practice, or research.

The last theme we observed in the empirical research relates to the very limited number of studies that integrated quantitative and qualitative research methods. In the early years of the charter movement with far fewer charters opened in a small number of states, we observed that the studies were fairly narrow in geographic coverage, typically focusing on exploratory single-case studies or at most several case studies within the same state or region of the state.

As the charter school population has expanded, a few researchers, most notably Margaret E. Raymond of the Center for Research on Education Outcomes (CREDO) at Stanford University, have explored conducting national studies of charter schools. Limitations in the availability of longitudinal student-level data led Raymond to create comparison groups for charter schools which she called "virtual twins" to measure charter school performance.[13] This new method used all available, observable charter student characteristics and prior performance to create a composite comparison record. Raymond's 2009 report on this study, "Multiple Choice: Charter School Performance in 16 States," was controversial because of its research methods and also was criticized because it shed little light on the diversity of charter schooling. While Raymond's report created a "sound bite" for detractors to point to the small percentage of charter schools outperforming non-charter public schools, the bigger takeaway was that since some charter schools are underperforming and others are outperforming comparison schools, we need to determine what accounts for the mixed results. Is it related to curriculum and instruction? What about the "toughness" of the authorizer? We have limited knowledge about what makes charter schools perform better or worse than comparison groups.

This theme suggests a new avenue of research devoted to figuring out what explains variations in school performance. How are charter schools using their autonomy and authority to finance, govern, and educate students, and to what extent do these variables and others (e.g., the age of the school) influence school performance? At this point, we still know incredibly little about the education inside the black box of schooling. Therefore, we encourage future research about charter schools to consider integrating quantitative and qualitative research methods from the study's start.

Let's take the example of California, where both the research community and the state charter school association closely monitor the performance of charter schools statewide. Several recent studies of California charter schools concluded that charters were overrepresented at the top of the distribution and at the low end.[14] Armed with this information, are there commonalities among charter schools in each of the two overrepresented groups? What are the elements of charter schooling associated with higher (and lower) academic performance—the no-excuses model, funding priorities, an intensive focus on traditional reading and math skills, extended time in school? Using qualitative methods to help inform the quantitative results would be the logical next step. For example, are there differences between what have been called mission-focused and market-focused charter schools? Or is that dichotomy too simplistic? Dick Carpenter of the University of Colorado at Colorado Springs, who once served as principal of a K–8 charter school, created a typology that arrays the charter school population related to the schools' instructional approaches or curriculum themes. Carpenter created his typology by sorting 1,182 charter schools, representing 87 percent of all those operating in 2001–2002 in the five states (Arizona, California, Florida, Michigan, and Texas) that then accounted for the lion's share of U.S. charter schools. Carpenter ultimately grouped charter schools into five categories: 1) traditional (e.g., Core Knowledge, back-to-basics); 2) progressive (e.g., Montessori and other project-based, hands-on approaches); 3) vocational (e.g., preparing students with the transition from school to work); 4) general (e.g., usually conversion schools with no distinct curricular or pedagogical emphasis); and 5) alternative delivery (e.g., cyber, blended learning charters).[15] Studies could assess whether these qualitatively different types of charter schools achieve quantitatively different outcomes.

While qualitative methods are being pursued to deepen knowledge about the black box, quantitative researchers can reenter to monitor charter performance. Do the same charter schools persist over time? That is, do the lowest performers remain in that group over years, or do some exit, for example, as the school ages? Similarly, at the top end of the performance distribution, how long do charter schools remain there? Do they exit when the founder departs? Qualitative researchers then can explore in more detail what characteristics are associated with the charters that stay and the ones that exit. Further, as researchers move forward to determine what variables are associated with charter school performance, we hope to see policies and practices that work disseminated more widely.

After considering the wide range of research we studied and the commentators we interviewed, we feel that charter schools will very likely remain a long-term fixture on the education landscape. The chapters stress our conclusion that charter schools have addressed, at least to some extent, all the legislated purposes for which they were created, although some of these purposes have been borne out more than others. Further, we found that research results evaluating the performance of charters within a single purpose were similarly diverse. The diversity of research results, combined with the observations of our commentators, can enrich learning and improvement in the charter sector. Our hope is that charter petitions in the future will be viewed as enablers of reform and not be emblematic of one kind of school. Our future work as researchers, policy makers, and practitioners will be to create and track what charter schools do with their petitions and what outcomes they achieve.

———■■■———

Notes on Research

THE NEED FOR A SYSTEMATIC REVIEW PROCESS

We modeled our systematic review of prior research after previous systematic literature reviews (see for example, EPPI-Center, Means et al.) and used as a framework the eight steps outlined in Petrosino and Lavenberg's work on conducting systematic reviews combined with Anfara, Brown, and Mangione's description of rigorous qualitative coding techniques.[1] Petrosino and Lavenberg identify the following eight steps in a systematic literature review:[2]

1. The question(s) guiding the work is explicit and can be answered by a systematic review.
2. The eligibility criteria for studies to be included is explicit.
3. The search methods are comprehensive and designed to reduce potential bias.
4. Each potentially eligible study is screened against the criteria with exclusions justified and recorded.
5. The sample of eligible studies and the corresponding data set is the most complete possible.
6. If meta-analysis is possible, the methods are technically appropriate.
7. If statistical analyses are used to examine subgroup effects, they are technically appropriate.
8. A structured and detailed report, explicitly reporting each stage of the review, is produced.

Because most research on charter schools did not employ experimental design, it was not possible to perform meta-analysis. Consequently, this study substituted Anfara, Brown, and Mangione's procedural approach to coding for steps 6 and 7.[3] This approach involves creating a map of the codes used in analysis to provide evidence of the process of theme development.

PHASE 1: WHAT'S IN, WHAT'S OUT

We began by collecting peer-reviewed journal articles published between January 1, 2000, and December 31, 2011. Studies were identified through six databases: What Works Clearinghouse, ProQuest, JSTOR, Educational Resources Information Center (ERIC), PsycInfo, and Education Abstracts. "Peer-reviewed" is defined "as the process through which experts in a field of study assess the quality of articles that are submitted to a journal for publication."[4] A preliminary search of the terms "charter school(s)" and "school choice" resulted in nearly 7,000 hits.

Given the lag time between research, journal submission, and publication, we also identified empirically based reports and studies self-published by research centers and think tanks from January 1, 2007, through December 31, 2011, in order to capture recent research that would not yet be available in peer-reviewed journals. We identified twenty-nine research centers, think tanks, and university research centers whose Web sites were searched for reports to screen for inclusion. After all potential articles were identified, we devised screening protocols based on the following inclusion/exclusion criteria:

- The publication is about charter schools in the United States.
- The publication presents new qualitative or quantitative empirical data and/or systematically reviews a body of existing empirical work.
- The study was published in a peer-reviewed journal or was self-published by a research center or think tank.

• Books and book chapters were excluded, since the findings from these sources generally also appear in peer-reviewed journals. Also excluded were commentaries, reports by partisan organizations, state/district indicator reports, dissertations, and external audit reports or EMO investment analysts' reports.

At the end of phase 1, of the original total hits, around 5,500 publications were excluded because they did not meet the inclusion criteria, and close to 1,000 were excluded because they were duplicates of articles already reviewed (e.g., the same article appearing in both ProQuest and JSTOR). Over 500 peer-reviewed journal articles and self-published reports were included for full-text review. After reviewing the full text of the documents that passed the first round of screening, additional publications were excluded for failing to meet the inclusion criteria, leaving close to 400 publications remaining.

We used ATLAS.ti, a qualitative research software program, to code and analyze included publications. We developed a code list to capture information relating to the study's research questions through an iterative process based on prior knowledge, team meetings, development of the conceptual framework, and expert advice. For example, codes designed to understand the landscape of prior research included publication type, study sample, research design, data collection methods, analysis conducted, data source, study limitations, and areas for future study. Additionally, we developed a codebook to ensure common understanding of each code's intended purpose. Each entry included the code label, definition, indicators, and exclusions.

To ensure inter-rater reliability, we conducted a pilot test of the code list and codebook by coding the same four articles. The results of the pilot coding were reviewed by the entire coding group to identify discrepancies and to clarify the meaning and application of codes. We amended the code list and book to reflect slight refinements, based on feedback from the pilot test. A second pilot test of four additional articles followed to ensure that codes were applied consistently. Throughout the coding process, we stayed in constant contact to address questions as they arose. Article coding was frequently checked by multiple team members to ensure that we maintained reliability.

PHASE 2: QUALITY RATINGS

While we wanted to be as comprehensive as possible, we recognized that not all research was designed and conducted with equal quality. We felt an imperative to distinguish between research that was of high quality and research that was not by applying accepted standards of quality.

While there is general consensus around experimental and quasi-experimental designs, there is less agreement on how to judge the quality of qualitative research approaches. Toward this end, as noted above, we examined literature reviews in a number of AERA outlets and developed a list of characteristics that when applied would help us sift through the studies to identify the ones of highest quality.[5] We devised a set of quality indicators that could be applied across both qualitative and quantitative research: study sample, study period, design and data collection methods, documentation of research methods, and triangulation of data sources. In addition, we verified that findings were supported by evidence and that studies addressed reliability, validity, and credibility issues based on the "Standards for Reporting on Empirical Social Science Research in AERA Publications."[6]

Of the articles that passed the initial screening (phase 1, above), we asked, what is their relative quality? To this end, we adopted a three-point scale: highest quality (3), medium quality (2), and lowest quality (1). We applied these standards regardless of the particular study methods, assigning one overall rating to each article. Specifically, we considered the following criteria:

- Clear problem formulation and purpose
- Review of relevant scholarship
- Transparent description of:

Research design
    Units of study and how selected
    Comparison groups
Data collection
    Time and duration of data collection
    Description of instruments
Data analysis
    Measurements/statistical analyses of data elements
    Appropriateness of analytic procedures
    Classification/coding schemes
    Triangulation across data sources
- Conclusion
    Claims and interpretations supported by evidence
    Discussion of generalizability—validity/reliability

Although we wanted to cast a wide net in our review, we agreed that our job as authors was to guide readers through the piles of studies on charter schools based on the quality of the research, in order to be able to distill credible recommendations for charter school policy, practice, and further research in this area. The quality review process enabled us to do this. Within the manuscript drafting, we chose to highlight those articles that had received the highest quality ranking.

NOTES

FOREWORD

1. For an overview of charter school politics see Michael W. Kirst, "Politics of Charter Schools: Competing National Advocacy Coalitions Meet Local Politics," *Peabody Journal of Education*, 82, nos. 2–3 (2007): 184–203.

2. Jeffrey Henig, *Spin Cycle: How Research Gets Used in Policy Debate* (New York: Russell Sage, 2008).

3. Michael Mintrom, *Policy Entrepreneurs and School Choice* (Washington, DC: Georgetown University, 2000).

4. Martin Carnoy, Rebecca Jacobsen, Lawrence Mishel, and Richard Rothstein, *The Charter School Dust-up* (Washington, DC: Economic Policy Institute, 2005).

5. For more details on these advocacy coalitions see Michael W. Kirst and Frederick M. Wirt, *Political Dynamics of American Education* (Richmond, CA: McCutchan, 2009), 333–53.

INTRODUCTION

1. National Center for Educational Statistics, "The Condition of Education 2012" (Washington, DC: U.S. Department of Education, 2012).

2. National Alliance for Public Charter Schools, "Back to School Tallies: Estimated Number of Public Charter Schools & Students, 2011–2012" (Washington, DC: National Alliance for Public Charter Schools, 2011).

3. Paul Hill and Christine Campbell, *Portfolio School Districts Project* (Seattle: Center on Reinventing Public Education, 2011).

4. William J. Bushaw and Shane J. Lopez Phi, "The 43rd Annual Phi Delta Kappa/Gallup Poll of the Public's Attitudes Toward Public Schools," *Phi Delta Kappan* 93, no. 1 (2011): 8–26.

5. Katrina Bulkley and Jennifer Fisler, "A Decade of Charter Schools: From Theory to Practice," *Educational Policy* 17, no. 3 (2007): 317–42.

6. National Center for Educational Statistics, "Condition of Education 2012."

7. Heather Staker, "The Rise of K–12 Blended Learning: Profiles of Emerging Models" (Mountain View, CA: Innosight Institute and Charter School Growth Fund, 2011).

8. See Priscilla Wohlstetter and Lesley Anderson, "What can U.S. charter schools learn from England's grant-maintained schools?" *Phi Delta Kappan* 75, no. 6 (1994): 486–91; Geoff Whitty, "Policy Tourism and Policy Borrowing: Why Does It Happen

and What Good Does It Do?" (lecture presented at Teachers College, Columbia University, Nov. 8, 2010).

9. Priscilla Wohlstetter, Amy N. Van Kirk, Peter J. Robertson, and Susan A. Mohrman, *Organizing for Successful School-Based Management* (Alexandria, VA: Association for Supervision and Curriculum Development, 1997); Priscilla Wohlstetter, Roxane Smyer, and Susan Mohrman, "New boundaries for school-based management: The high-involvement model," *Educational Evaluation and Policy Analysis* 16, no. 3 (1994): 268–86.

10. Susan Fuhrman and Richard Elmore, *Redesigning Accountability Systems for Education* (New York: Teachers College Press, 2004).

11. Tim L. Mazzoni, "The changing politics of state education policymaking: A 20-year Minnesota perspective," *Educational Evaluation and Policy Analysis* 15, no. 4 (1993): 357–79; Nancy C. Roberts and Paula J. King, *Transforming Public Policy: Dynamics of Policy Entrepreneurship and Innovation* (San Francisco: Jossey-Bass Publishers, 1996).

12. The Friedman Foundation for Educational Choice, "What is School Choice?" www.edchoice.org.

13. Ted Kolderie, "Ray Budde and the Origins of the Charter Concept" (Minneapolis: Education Evolving, 2005), http://www.educationevolving.org/pdf/Ray_Budde.pdf.

14. Ray Budde, "Education by Charter: Restructuring school districts: Key to long-term continuing improvement for American education," *Phi Delta Kappan* 70, no. 7 (1989): 518–20.

15. Ted Kolderie, "How the Idea of 'Chartering' Schools Came About," *Minnesota Journal* 25, no. 5 (2008): 5–6.

16. For more information please see Ember Reichgott Junge, *Zero Chance of Passage: The Pioneering Charter School Story* (Edina, MN: Beaver's Pond Press, 2012).

17. Minnesota Charter Schools Association, "MN Association of Charter Schools," http://www.mncharterschools.org.

18. EdSource: Engaging Californians on Key Education Challenges, "Charter School History and Policy," www.edsource.org/iss_charter_policy.html.

19. Priscilla Wohlstetter, Nicole Griffin, and Derrick Chau, "Charter schools in California: A bruising campaign for public school choice," in *The Charter School Landscape*, ed. S. Vergari (Pittsburgh: University of Pittsburgh Press, 2002).

20. Mazzoni, "Changing politics."

21. Louann Bierlein Palmer and Rebecca Gau, "Charter School Authorizing Policy Implications from a National Study," *Phi Delta Kappan* 86, no. 5 (2005).

22. Gregg Vanourek, Bruno V. Manno, and Chester E. Finn Jr., "The False Friends of Charter Schools," *Education Week* 16, no. 31 (1997).

23. Alex Medler and Joe Nathan, "Charter Schools . . . What Are They Up To? A 1995 Survey" (Denver: Education Commission of the States, 1995).

24. Beryl Nelson, Paul Berman, John Ericson, Nancy Kamprath, Rebecca Perry, Debi Silverman, and Debra Solomon,"The state of charter schools, 2000: Fourth-year report" (Washington, DC: U.S. Department of Education, 2009).

25. Caitlin C. Farrell, Priscilla Wohlstetter, and Joanna Smith, "Charter

management organizations: An emerging approach to scaling up what works," *Educational Policy* 26, no. 4 (2012): 499–532; Robin Lake, Brianna Dusseault, Melissa Bowen, Allison Demeritt, and Paul Hill, "The national study of charter management organization effectiveness: Report on interim findings" (Seattle: Mathematica Policy Research and Center on Reinventing Public Education, 2010).

26. National Alliance for Public Charter Schools, "Charter school caps," www.publiccharters.org/files/publications/Charter_School_Caps.pdf.

27. Erik W. Robelen, "State legislatures wrestle with charter laws," *Education Week* 28, no. 37 (2009).

28. U.S. Department of Education, "Race To The Top," http://racetotop.com.

29. Education|Evolving, "A Model RFP" (Saint Paul, MN: The Center for Policy Studies, 2004).

30. National Alliance for Public Charter Schools, "Measuring Up to the Model: A Tool for Comparing State Charter School Laws," http://www.publiccharters.org/law.

31. National Association of Charter School Authorizers, "Principles and Standards for Quality Charter School Authorizing" (Chicago: National Association of Charter School Authorizers, 2010).

32. National Association of Charter School Authorizers, "The Fund for Authorizing Excellence," www.qualitycharters.org.

33. Associated Press, "Number of Students in Charters Rises," *Education Week* 31, no. 14 (2011): 4.

34. U.S. Department of Education, "Charter Schools Program Grants for Replication and Expansion of High Quality Charter Schools," www2.ed.gov/programs/charter-rehqcs/index.html.

35. Michelle McNeil, "49 applicants win 'i3' grants," *Education Week,* August 4, 2010, www.blogs.edweek.org/edweek/campaign-k-12/2010/08/49_applicants_win_i3_grants_1.html.

36. The Bill and Melinda Gates Foundation, "Five California Public Charter Networks Receive $60 Million to Promote Effective Teaching and Prepare More Students to Succeed in College," www.thecollegereadypromise.org.

37. The Broad Foundation, "The Broad Prize for Public Charter Schools," www.broadprize.org.

38. Joshua Furgeson, Brian Gill, Joshua Haimson, Alexandra Killewald, Moira McCullough, Ira Nichols-Barrer, Bing-ru Teh, Natalya Verbitsky-Savitz, Melissa Bowen, Allison Demeritt, Paul Hill, and Robin Lake, "Charter-school management organizations: Diverse strategies and diverse student impacts" (Seattle: University of Washington and Mathematica Policy Research, 2012).

39. Beth Hawkins, "Ted Kolderie, nationally honored education innovator, explains why school change is so hard," *MinnPost,* August 19, 2011.

40. Paul T. O'Neill and Todd Ziebarth, eds., *Charter School Law Deskbook,* 2008–2009 Edition (Charlottesville, VA: LexisNexis, 2009).

41. Andy Smarick, "Original Intent: What legislative history tells us about the purposes of chartering" (unpublished, 2005).

42. O'Neill and Ziebarth, *Charter School Law Deskbook.*

43. Ibid.

44. Elizabeth A. Butler, Joanna Smith, and Priscilla Wohlstetter, "Creating and sustaining high-quality charter school governing boards" (Washington, DC: National Resource Center on Charter School Finance and Governance, 2008); Chuan A. Kuzin, "Parent compacts in urban charter schools: An exploration of contents and processes" (PhD dissertation, University of Southern California, 2012).

45. O'Neill and Ziebarth, *Charter School Law Deskbook.*

46. Ibid.

47. For a more complete discussion of the literature review methods, please see Joanna Smith, Priscilla Wohlstetter, Caitlin Farrell, and Michelle Nayfack, "Beyond Ideological Warfare: The Maturation of Research on Charter Schools," *Journal of School Choice* 5, no. 4 (2011): 444–507.

48. Alison Consoletti, "The State of Charter Schools: What We Know—and What We Do Not—About Performance and Accountability" (Washington, DC: Center for Education Reform, 2011); National Association of Charter School Authorizers, "The State of Charter School Authorizing: Fourth Annual Report on NACSA's Authorizer Survey 2011" (Chicago: NACSA, 2012).

CHAPTER ONE

1. Florida, *Florida Statutes*, "Education Code" (1996) § 1002.33.

2. Marisa Cannata, "Charter schools and the teacher job search," *Journal of School Choice* 5, no. 1 (2011): 111–33.

3. Susan Bowles Therriault, Allison Gruner Gandhi, Julie Casasanto, and Samantha Carney, "Out of the debate and into the schools: Comparing practices and strategies in traditional, pilot and charter schools in the city of Boston" (Washington, DC: American Institutes for Research, 2010).

4. Julia E. Koppich, Patricia Holmes, and Margaret L. Plecki, *New Rules, New Roles? The Professional Work Lives of Charter School Teachers. A Preliminary Study* (Annapolis, MD: NEA Professional Library, 1998); Bruce D. Baker and Jill L. Dickerson, "Charter schools, teacher labor market deregulation, and teacher quality: Evidence from the Schools and Staffing Survey," *Educational Policy* 20, no. 5 (2006); Marisa Cannata, "Teacher Qualifications and Work Environments Across School Types," in *School Choice: Evidence and Recommendations*, ed. Gary Miron et al. (Boulder, CO: Education Policy Research Unit and Education and the Public Interest Center, 2008); Debbi C. Harris, "Should I Stay or Should I Go? Comparing Teacher Mobility in Florida's Charter and Traditional Public Schools," *Peabody Journal of Education* 82, no. 2/3 (2007).

5. Richard S. Brown, Priscilla Wohlstetter, and Sunny Liu, "Developing an Indicator System for Schools of Choice: A Balanced Scorecard Approach," *Journal of School Choice* 2, no. 4 (2008): 392–414.

6. Center on Educational Governance, "2010 Charter Schools Indicators," University of Southern California, Rossier School of Education (2010), http://www.uscrossier.org/ceg.

7. Courtney L. Malloy and Priscilla Wohlstetter, "Working conditions in charter schools: What's the appeal for teachers?," *Education and Urban Society* 35, no. 2 (2003).

8. Ibid.

9. Gary Miron and Brooks Applegate, "Teacher attrition in charter schools" (Boulder, CO: Education Policy Research Unit and Education and the Public Interest Center, 2007); David Stuit and Thomas Smith, "Teacher turnover in charter schools" (Nashville, TN: National Center on School Choice, 2009); Thomas Smith and Richard Ingersoll, "What are the effects of induction and mentoring on beginning teacher turnover?," *American Educational Research Journal* 41, no. 3 (2004): 681–714; Linda A. Renzulli, Heather Macpherson Parrott, and Irenee R. Beattie, "Racial mismatch and school type: Teacher satisfaction and retention in charter and traditional public schools," *Sociology of Education* 84, no. 1 (2011): 23–48; Betheny Gross and Michael DeArmond, "How do charter schools compete for teachers? A local perspective," *Journal of School Choice* 4, no. 3 (2010): 254–77.

10. Harris, "Should I Stay or Should I Go?"

11. Miron and Applegate, "Teacher attrition."

12. Stuit and Smith, "Teacher turnover."

13. Smith and Ingersoll, "Effects of induction and mentoring?"

14. Gross and DeArmond, "How do charter schools compete?"

15. Michael Lipsky, *Street-level Bureaucracy: Dilemmas of the Individual in Public Services* (New York: Russell Sage Foundation, 1980).

16. Joanna Smith, Priscilla Wohlstetter, and Dominic J. Brewer, "Under new management: Are charter schools making the most of new governance options?" (Seattle: Center on Reinventing Public Education, 2007), 19.

17. Anthony Milanowski, "The varieties of knowledge and skill-based pay design: A comparison of seven new pay systems for K–12 teachers," http://epaa.asu.edu/ojs/article/view/232.

18. Michael DeArmond, Betheny Gross, and Dan Goldhaber, "Look familiar? Charters and teachers" (Seattle: Center on Reinventing Public Education, 2007).

19. Gross and DeArmond, "How do charter schools compete?"

20. Eileen M. Kellor, "Catching up with the Vaughn express: Six years of standards-based teacher evaluation and performance pay," *Education Policy Analysis Archives* 13, no. 7 (2005): 11.

21. Ibid, 5.

22. Lan Hue Quach, "A paradox of care: [Re]-examining education for students with diverse needs," *Educational Foundations* 19, no. 1–2 (2005); Babette M. Benken and Nancy Brown, "Moving beyond the barriers: A re-defined, multi-leveled partnership approach to mathematics teacher education," *Issues in Teacher Education* 17, no. 2 (2008): 63–82.

23. Marjorie Clark, "Finding balance: The professional life of a charter school teacher," *Teacher Education and Practice* 23, no. 2 (2010): 210–25.

24. Marisa Cannata, "Teacher Community in Elementary Charter Schools," *Education Policy Analysis Archives* 15, no. 11 (2007).

25. Katrina E. Bulkley and Jennifer Hicks, "Managing community: Professional community in charter schools operated by educational management organizations," *Educational Administration Quarterly* 41, no. 2 (2005).

26. See Cannata, "Teacher Community"; Malloy and Wohlstetter, "Working

conditions in charter schools"; Patricia L. Marshall, Drena C. Gibbs, Tammy M. Greene, William C. Nelson, and Jamie R. Schofield, "Teachers reflect on charter schools," *Kappa Delta Pi Record* 37, no. 3 (2001); Scott Milliman and Robert Maranto, "Educational Renegades: Dissatisfied Teachers as Drivers of Charter School Formation," *Journal of School Choice* 3, no. 2 (2009); Michael Mintrom, "Market organizations and deliberative democracy: Choice and voice in public service delivery," *Administration & Society* 35, no. 1 (2003); Julie Landry Petersen, "Learning Facts: The Brave New World of Data-Informed Instruction," *Education Next* 7, no. 1 (2007); Quach, "Paradox of care."

27. Petersen, "Learning Facts," 39.

28. Ron Zimmer and Richard Buddin, "Getting inside the black box: Examining how the operation of charter schools affects performance," *Peabody Journal of Education* 82, no. 2 (2007).

29. Noelle C. Griffin and Priscilla Wohlstetter, "Building a plane while flying it: Early lessons from developing charter schools," *Teachers College Record* 103, no. 2 (2001).

30. Heath Brown, "Incentives in U.S. charter schools: For-profit and nonprofit choices," *Journal of School Choice* 2, no. 4 (2008): 415–39; Baker and Dickerson, "Charter schools, teacher labor market deregulation, and teacher quality."

31. Ibid; Bulkley and Hicks, "Managing community"; Cannata, "Teacher Qualifications"; J. Christensen and R. J. Lake, "The national charter school landscape in 2007" (Seattle: Center on Reinventing Public Education, 2007); Carrie Y. Barron Ausbrooks, Edith J. Barrett, and Theresa Daniel, "Texas charter school legislation and the evolution of open-enrollment charter schools," *Education Policy Analysis Archives* 13, no. 21 (2005).

CHAPTER TWO

1. Alex Medler and Joe Nathan, *Charter Schools . . . What Are They Up To? A 1995 Survey* (Denver: Education Commission of the States, 1995).

2. Mary Bailey Estes, "Choice for All? Charter Schools and Students with Special Needs," *Journal of Special Education* 37, no. 4 (2004); Margaret McLaughlin, Kelly Henderson, and Hafeez Ullah, *Charter Schools and Students with Disabilities* (Alexandria, VA: Center for Policy and Research, 1996); Betsy Levin, "Race and school choice," in *School Choice and Social Controversy*, eds. Stephen D. Sugarman and Frank R. Kemerer (Washington, DC: Brookings Institution Press, 1999), 266–99; Lauren Rhim and Margaret J. McLaughlin, "Charter Schools and Special Education: Balancing Disparate Visions" (Alexandria, VA: National Association of State Directors of Special Education, 2000).

3. Ron Zimmer and Richard Buddin, "Getting inside the black box: Examining how the operation of charter schools affects performance," *Peabody Journal of Education* 82, no. 2–3 (2007).

4. C. Y. B. Ausbrooks, E. J. Barrett, and T. Daniel, "Texas charter school legislation and the evolution of open-enrollment charter schools."

5. Zimmer and Buddin, "Getting inside the black box."

6. Roslyn Arlin Mickelson, Martha Bottia, and Stephanie Southworth, "School

Choice and Segregation by Race, Class, and Achievement," in *School Choice: Evidence and Recommendations*, eds. Gary Miron et al. (Boulder: Education Policy Research Unit and Education and the Public Interest Center, 2008); Lan Hue Quach, "A paradox of care: [Re]-examining education for students with diverse needs," *Educational Foundations* 19, no. 1–2 (2005); Joe Nathan and William L. Boyd, "Lessons about School Choice from Minnesota: Promise and Challenges," *Phi Delta Kappan* 84, no. 5 (2003); Jeffrey Henig and Jason A. MacDonald, "Locational decisions of charter schools: Probing the market metaphor," *Social Science Quarterly* 83, no. 4 (2002).

7. Culter, "City Academy: A Charter School Prototype," *Phi Delta Kappan* 78, no. 1 (1996): 26–27.

8. Kevin Booker, Tim R. Sass, Brian Gill, and Ron Zimmer, "Going Beyond Test Scores—Evaluating Charter School Impact on Educational Attainment in Chicago and Florida" (New York: National Center for the Study of Privatization in Education, 2008).

9. Grace Calisi Corbett and Tracy A. Huebner, "Rethinking High School: Preparing students for success in college, career, and life," in *Rethinking High School*, ed. Joy Zimmerman (San Francisco: WestEd, 2007).

10. Betheny Gross and Kirsten Martens Pochop, "How Charter Schools Organize for Instruction," in *Hopes, Fears and Reality: A Balanced Look at American Charter Schools in 2008*, ed. Robin J. Lake (Seattle: National Charter School Research Project and the Center on Reinventing Public Education, 2008), 9–22.

11. Raquel L. Farmer-Hinton, "On Becoming College Prep: Examining the Challenges Charter School Staff Members Face While Executing a School's Mission," *Teachers College Record* 108, no. 6 (2006); Raquel L. Farmer-Hinton and Ruanda Garth McCullough, "College counseling in charter schools: Examining the opportunities and challenges," *High School Journal* 9, no. 4 (2008): 77–90.

12. Sarah Yatsko, Betheny Gross, and Jon Christensen, "Charter high schools: Alternative paths to graduation," in *White Paper Series, No. 3*, ed. National Charter School Research Project (Seattle: Center for Reinventing Public Education, 2009).

13. Meg Gebhard, "Charter Schools and Bilingual Education: A Case Study of Teachers Negotiating Policy-Making Roles," *Equity & Excellence in Education* 35, no. 3 (2002); Letitia Basford, Sarah Hick, and Martha Bigelow, "Educating Muslims in an east African US charter high school" (New York: National Center for the Study of Privatization in Education, 2007); Elizabeth K. Davenport and Yolanda K. H. Bogan, "It takes a village to teach a child: An analysis of an African-centered parent involvement program," *AASA Journal of Scholarship and Practice* 2, no. 3 (2005); J. Kay Fenimore-Smith, "The Power of Place: Creating an Indigenous Charter School," *Journal of American Indian Education* 48, no. 2 (2009); Kate Anderson Simons and Patrick A. Curtis, "Connecting with Communities: Four Successful Schools," *Young Children* 62, no. 2 (2007).

14. Quach, "Paradox of care."

15. Jon Christensen and Lydia Rainey, "Custom tailored: Trends in charter school educational programs," in *Inside Charter Schools* (Seattle: Center on Reinventing Public Education, 2009).

16. Ibid.

17. Gross and Martens Pochop, "How Charter Schools Organize."

18. Margaret Raymond, "Paying for A's: An Early Exploration of Student Reward and Incentive Programs in Charter Schools," in Center for Research on Education Outcomes (Palo Alto, CA: Stanford University, 2008).

19. Caroline M. Hoxby and Sonali Murarka, "New York City Charter Schools," *Education Next* 8, no. 3 (2008); Caroline M. Hoxby, Sonali Murarka, and Jenny Kang, *How New York City's Charter Schools Affect Achievement, August 2009 Report* (Cambridge, MA: New York City Charter Schools Evaluation Project, 2009).

20. Michael Mintrom, "Market organizations and deliberative democracy: Choice and voice in public service delivery," *Administration & Society* 35, no. 1 (2003).

21. Jon Christensen and Robin J. Lake, "The national charter school landscape in 2007" (Seattle: Center on Reinventing Public Education, 2007), 7.

22. Judit Szente, "Teleconferencing across borders: Promoting literacy—and more—in the elementary grades," *Childhood Education* 79, no. 5 (2003).

23. Richard Neumann, "Charter Schools and Innovation: The High Tech High Model," *American Secondary Education* 36, no. 3 (2008).

24. Luis A. Huerta, Mana-Fernanda Gonzalez, and Chad d'Entremont, "Cyber and Home School Charter Schools: Adopting Policy to New Forms of Public Schooling," *Peabody Journal of Education* 81, no. 1 (2006).

25. Ibid.

26. Carol Klein and Mary Poplin, "Families Home Schooling in a Virtual Charter School System," *Marriage & Family Review* 43, no. 3/4 (2008); Rose M. Marsh, Allison A. Carr-Chellman, and Beth R. Sockman, "Selecting Silicon: Why Parents Choose Cybercharter Schools," *TechTrends* 53, no. 4 (2009).

27. Shellie Hipsky and Lindsay Adams, "Strategies for teaching students with exceptional needs in cyber schools," *International Journal of Information and Communication Technology Education* 2, no. 4 (2006).

28. Lisa M. Shoaf, "Perceived advantages and disadvantages of an online charter school," *The American Journal of Distance Education* 21, no. 4 (2007).

29. Zimmer and Buddin, "Getting inside the black box."

30. Klein and Poplin, "Families Home Schooling."

31. Shoaf, "Perceived advantages and disadvantages."

32. Ron Zimmer, Brian Gill, Kevin Booker, Stéphane Lavertu, Tim R. Sass, and John Witte, "Charter Schools in Eight States: Effects on Achievement, Attainment, Integration, and Competition" (Santa Monica, CA: RAND Corporation, 2009).

33. Todd Ziebarth, Mary Beth Celio, Robin J. Lake, and Lydia Rainey, "The charter schools landscape in 2005," in *Hopes, Fears, and Reality: A Balanced Look at American Charter Schools in 2005*, (eds.) R. J. Lake and P. T. Hill (Seattle: National Charter School Research Project, 2005), 1–20.

34. Priscilla Wohlstetter, Courtney L. Malloy, Guilbert C. Hentschke, and Joanna Smith, "Improving service delivery in education through collaboration: An exploratory study of the role of cross-sectoral alliances in the development and support of charter schools," *Social Science Quarterly* 85, no. 5 (2004).

35. Jan Lacina, Lysa Hagan, and Becky Griffith, "Developing a Writing Workshop Classroom: Collaboration Between a Charter School Principal, Second-Grade Teacher, and University Professor," *The Teacher Educator* 42, no. 1 (2006).

36. Joanna Smith, Priscilla Wohlstetter, and Guilbert C. Hentschke, "A Guide for State Policymakers: Partnerships Between Charter Schools and Other Organizations" (Washington, DC: National Resource Center on Charter School Finance and Governance, 2008); Wohlstetter et al., "Improving service delivery."

37. Priscilla Wohlstetter, Courtney L. Malloy, Joanna Smith, and Guilbert C. Hentshke, "Incentives for charter schools: Building school capacity through cross-sectoral alliances," *Educational Administration Quarterly* 40, no. 3 (2004).

38. Smith, Wohlstetter, and Hentschke, "Partnerships between charter schools"; Wohlstetter et al., "Incentives for charter schools."

39. Smith, Wohlstetter, and Hentschke, "Partnerships between charter schools"; Wohlstetter et al., "Improving service delivery."

40. Christopher Lubienski, "Innovation in education markets: Theory and evidence on the impact of competition and choice in charter schools," *American Educational Research Journal* 40, no. 2 (2003).

41. Ibid.

42. Ibid.

43. Ausbrooks, Barrett, and Daniel, "Texas charter school legislation"; Christopher Lubienski, "Incentives for School Diversification: Competition and Promotional Patterns in Local Education Markets," *Journal of School Choice* 1 (2006): 1–31; Yatsko, Gross, and Christensen, "Alternative paths."

44. Ausbrooks, Barrett, and Daniel, "Texas charter school legislation," 15–16.

45. Yatsko, Gross, and Christensen, "Alternative paths."

46. Joanna Smith, Priscilla Wohlstetter, and Dominic J. Brewer, "Under new management: Are charter schools making the most of new governance options?" (Seattle: Center on Reinventing Public Education, 2007), 17–27.

47. Ibid, 18.

48. Lubienski, "Innovation in education markets"; Peter McDermott, Julia Johnson Rothenberg, and Kim Baker, "Lessons Learned from the First Year of an Urban Charter School," *The Educational Forum* 70, no. 4 (2006); Katherine Merseth, *Inside Urban Charter Schools: Promising Practices and Strategies in Five High-Performing Schools* (Cambridge, MA: Harvard Education Press, 2009).

49. Joshua M. Cowen, David J. Fleming, and Anat Gofen, "Measuring the motivation to charter: An examination of school sponsors in Texas," *Journal of School Choice* 2, no. 2 (2008): 301–15; M. DeArmond, B. Gross, and D. Goldhaber, "Look familiar? Charters and teachers" (Seattle: Center on Reinventing Public Education, 2007), 43–51.

50. Raymond, "Paying for A's."

51. Center on Educational Governance, "Promising Practices Compendium Highlighting Innovations in Charter Schools," www.uscrossier.org/ceg/products-and-services/promising-practices-compendium.

52. Booker et al., "Going Beyond Test Scores"; Christensen and Rainey, "Custom tailored"; Reino Makkonen, Chun-Wei Huang, and Paul Koehler, "An analysis of

Utah's K–3 Reading Improvement Program," in *Issues & Answers* (Washington, DC: U.S. Department of Education, 2007).

CHAPTER THREE

1. Tennessee, *Tennessee Code Annotated,* "Tennessee Public Charter Schools Act" (2002) § 49-13-102; New York, *New York Statues,* "New York Education," § 2850.

2. J. R. Betts and Y. E. Tang, "Value-added and experimental studies on the effects of charter schools on student achievement" (Seattle: Center on Reinventing Public Education, 2008), 1.

3. Center for Research on Education Outcomes, "Multiple Choice: Charter School Performance in Sixteen States," (Palo Alto, CA: Center for Research on Education Outcomes, 2009), 3.

4. Caroline Hoxby and Sonali Murarka, "New York City Charter Schools," *Education Next* 8, no. 3 (2008).

5. Ron Zimmer and Richard Buddin, "Charter school performance in two large urban districts," *Journal of Urban Economics* 60, no. 2 (2006); Gary Wolfram, "Effect of time spent in charter schools on student test scores: A Michigan case study," *Journal of School Choice* 2, no. 1 (2008): 20–46; Kerry A. King, "Charter schools in Arizona: Does being a for-profit institution make a difference?," *Journal of Economic Issues* 4, no. 3 (2007): 729–46; CREDO, "Charter School Performance in Sixteen States."

6. Center for Research on Education Outcomes, "Charter School Performance in New York City" (Palo Alto, CA: CREDO, 2010).

7. CREDO, "Charter School Performance in Sixteen States."

8. King, "Charter schools in Arizona"; Wolfram, "Effect of time spent."

9. Christopher Lubienski and Sarah Theule Lubienski, "Charter schools, academic achievement and NCLB," *Journal of School Choice* 1, no. 3 (2006): 683.

10. Kim Bancroft, "To Have and to Have Not: The Socioeconomics of Charter Schools," *Education and Urban Society* 41, no. 2 (2009).

11. Comfort O. Okpala, Genniver C. Bell, and Kwami Tuprah, "A Comparative Study of Student Achievement in Traditional Schools and Schools of Choice in North Carolina," *Urban Education* 42, no. 4 (2006).

12. James L. Chamberlin, "Poverty, School Size and Charter Designation as Predictors of Student Achievement on a Statewide High-Stakes Testing Program," *AASA Journal of Scholarship & Practice* 4, no. 1 (2007).

13. CREDO, "Charter School Performance in Sixteen States."

14. June E. Downing, Sally Spencer, and Claire Cavallaro, "The Development of an Inclusive Charter Elementary School: Lessons Learned," *Research and Practice for Persons with Severe Disabilities* 29, no. 1 (2004).

15. Zimmer and Buddin, "Charter school performance."

16. Brian Edwards, Heather Barondess, and Eric Crane, "California's Charter Schools: Charters vs. Non-Charters" (Mountain View, CA: EdSource, 2009).

17. Kevin Booker, Brian Gill, Ron Zimmer, and Tim R. Sass, "Achievement and Attainment in Chicago Charter Schools" (Santa Monica, CA: RAND Corporation, 2009).

18. Betts and Tang, "Value-added and experimental studies."

19. Ron Zimmer, Suzanne Blanc, Brian Gill, and Jolley Christman, "Evaluating the performance of Philadelphia's charter schools" (Santa Monica, CA: RAND Corporation, 2008).

20. Ron Zimmer, Brian Gill, Kevin Booker, Stephen Lavertu, Tim R. Soss, and John Witte, "Charter schools in eight states: Effects on achievement, attainment, integration, and competition" (Santa Monica, CA: RAND Corporation, 2009).

21. Katrina Bulkley and Jennifer Fisler, "A decade of charter schools: From theory to practice," *Educational Policy* 17, no. 3 (2003): 317–42.

22. CREDO, "Charter School Performance in Sixteen States."

23. Ibid.

24. Zimmer et al., "Charter schools in eight states."

25. Zimmer et al., "Evaluating the performance."

26. Scott A. Imberman, "Achievement and Behavior in Charter Schools: Drawing a More Complete Picture" (New York: National Center for the Study for Privatization of Education, 2007).

27. Zimmer et al., "Charter schools in eight states."

28. Imberman, "Drawing a More Complete Picture."

29. Booker et al., "Achievement and Attainment"; Robert Bifulco and Helen F. Ladd, "Results from the Tar Heel state: Older students did better when in regular public schools," *Education Next 5*, no. 4 (2005); Zimmer et al., "Charter schools in eight states."

30. Bifulco and Ladd, "Results from the Tar Heel state."

31. Ibid, 63.

32. Ibid.

33. Zimmer et al., "Charter schools in eight states."

34. Wolfram, "Effect of time spent."

35. Zimmer et al., "Evaluating the performance."

36. Ibid.

37. Zimmer et al., "Charter schools in eight states."

38. Zimmer et al., "Charter schools in eight states."

39. Stephen B. Lawton, "Effective charter schools and charter school systems," *Planning and Changing* 40, no. 1/2 (2009).

40. Richard Buddin and Ron Zimmer, "Student achievement in charter schools: A complex picture," *Journal of Policy Analysis and Management* 24, no. 2 (2005).

41. Imberman, "Drawing a More Complete Picture."

42. Gary Miron, Stephanie Evergreen, and Jessica Urschel, "The Impact of School Choice Reforms on Student Achievement," in *School Choice: Evidence and Recommendations*, eds. Gary Miron et al. (Boulder, CO: Education Policy Research Unit and Education and the Public Interest Center, 2008).

43. CREDO, "Charter School Performance in Sixteen States"; Miron, Evergreen, and Urschel, "Impact of School Choice Reforms."

44. Betts and Tang, "Value-added and experimental studies"; Robert Bifulco and Helen F. Ladd, "Institutional Change and Coproduction of Public Services: The Effect of Charter Schools on Parental Involvement," *Journal of Public Administration Research and Theory* 16, no. 4 (2006).

45. Caroline M. Hoxby and Jonah E. Rockoff, "Findings from the city of big shoulders: Younger students learn more in charter schools," *Education Next 5*, no. 4 (2005): 58.

46. Betts and Tang, "Value-added and experimental studies."

47. Miron, Evergreen, and Urschel, "Impact of School Choice Reforms."

48. CREDO, "Charter School Performance in New York City"; CREDO, "Charter School Performance in Sixteen States"; Bifulco and Ladd, "Institutional Change."

49. CREDO, "Charter School Performance in Sixteen States"; Bifulco and Ladd, "Institutional Change."

50. CREDO, "Charter Schol Performance in Sixteen States."

51. Bifulco and Ladd, "Results from the Tar Heel state," 64.

52. Wolfram, "Effect of time spent."

53. Stéphane Lavertu and John Witte, "The impact of Milwaukee charter schools on student achievement," in *Issues in Governance Studies* (Washington, DC: The Brookings Institute, 2009), 1.

54. Zimmer et al., "Evaluating the performance."

55. Bifulco and Ladd, "Results from the Tar Heel state," 64.

56. Lavertu and Witte, "Impact of Milwaukee charter schools," 2.

57. Jeffrey R. Henig, "What Do We Know About the Outcomes of KIPP Schools?" (Boulder, CO: Education Policy Research Unit and Education and the Public Interest Center, 2008).

58. Ibid, 1.

59. Center on Educational Governance, "School Performance Dashboard 2012" (Los Angeles: CEG, 2012); *U.S. News & World Report*, "National Rankings: Best High Schools," July 6, 2012, www.usnews.com/education/best-high-schools/national-rankings.

60. The Preuss School, "Fact Sheet," June 28, 2012, www.preuss.ucsd.edu.

61. Kevin Booker, Tim R. Sass, Brian Gill, and Ron Zimmer, "Going Beyond Test Scores: Evaluating Charter School Impact on Educational Attainment in Chicago and Florida" (New York: National Center for the Study of Privatization in Education, 2008); Zimmer et al., "Charter schools in eight states."

62. Booker et al., "Achievement and Attainment"; Zimmer et al., "Charter schools in eight states"; Booker et al., "Going Beyond Test Scores."

63. Edith J. Barrett, "Evaluating Education Reform: Students' Views of Their Charter School Experience," *Journal of Educational Research* 96, no. 6 (2003); Douglas Lee Lauen, "To Choose or Not to Choose: High School Choice and Graduation in Chicago," *Educational Evaluation & Policy Analysis* 31, no. 3 (2009); Booker et al., "Achievement and Attainment"; John Bohte, "Examining the impact of charter schools on performance in traditional public schools," *Policy Studies Journal* 32, no. 4 (2004); Janelle Scott and Adriana Villavicencio, "School Context and Charter School Achievement: A Framework for Understanding the Performance 'Black Box,'" *Peabody Journal of Education* 84, no. 2 (2009); Booker et al., "Going Beyond Test Scores."

64. Margaret Raymond, "Paying for A's: An Early Exploration of Student Reward and Incentive Programs in Charter Schools," in *CREDO* (Palo Alto, CA:

Stanford University, 2008); Betts and Tang, "Value-added and experimental studies"; Zimmer et al., "Charter schools in eight states"; Kenneth Wong and Francis Shen, "Assessing Charter School Performance in Illinois: A Pilot Study Using Error-Band Analysis" (Nashville, TN: National Center on School Choice, 2007); Jennifer Jellison Holme and Meredith P. Richards, "School Choice and Stratification in a Regional Context: Examining the Role of Inter-District Choice," *Peabody Journal of Education* 84, no. 2 (2009); Scott and Villavicencio, "School Context."

65. Finch, Lapsley, and Baker-Boudissa, "Survival Analysis"; Hoxby and Rockoff, "Findings from the city of big shoulders"; Booker et al., "Going Beyond Test Scores"; Imberman, "Drawing a More Complete Picture"; Lavertu and Witte, "Impact of Milwaukee charter schools"; Miron, Evergreen, and Urschel, "Impact of School Choice Reforms"; Bifulco and Ladd, "Institutional Change"; Betts and Tang, "Value-added and experimental studies"; Martin H. Malin and Charles Taylor Kerchner, "Charter schools and collective bargaining: Compatible marriage or illegitimate relationship?" *Harvard Journal of Law and Public Policy* 30, no. 3 (2007); Lauren Morando Rhim and Margaret McLaughlin, "Students with Disabilities in Charter Schools: What We Now Know," *Focus on Exceptional Children* 39, no. 5 (2007); Scott and Villavicencio, "School Context"; Wolfram, "Effect of time spent"; Ronald Opp, Lynne M. Hamer, and Svetlana Beltyukova, "The utility of an involvement and talent development framework in defining charter school success: A pilot study," *Education and Urban Society* 34, no. 3 (2002).

66. Zimmer et al., "Charter schools in eight states"; Buddin and Zimmer, "Complex picture"; Heath Brown, "Incentives in U.S. charter schools: For-profit and nonprofit choices."

CHAPTER FOUR

1. Katrina Bulkley and Jennifer Fisler, "A decade of charter schools: From theory to practice," *Educational Policy* 17, no. 3 (2003): 317–42; K. S. Finnigan, "Charter school autonomy: The mismatch between theory and practice," *Educational Policy* 21, no. 3 (2007); Courtney L. Malloy and Priscilla Wohlstetter, "Working conditions in charter schools: What's the appeal for teachers?" *Education and Urban Society* 35, no. 2 (2003).

2. Jason Margolis, "'Every day I spin these plates': A case study of teachers amidst the charter phenomenon," *Educational Foundations* 19, no. 1/2 (2005).

3. WestEd, "Charter high schools closing the achievement gap: Innovations in education" (Washington, DC: U.S. Department of Education Office of Innovation and Improvement, 2006); WestEd, "Innovations in education: Successful charter schools" (Washington, DC: U.S. Department of Education Office of Innovation and Improvement, 2004).

4. WestEd, "Charter high schools closing"; WestEd, "Innovations in education."

5. Sarah Yatsko, Betheny Gross, and Jon Christensen, "Charter high schools: Alternative paths to graduation," in *White Paper Series No. 3*, ed. National Charter School Research Project (Seattle: Center for Reinventing Public Education, 2009).

6. Roslyn Arlin Mickelson, Martha Bottia, and Stephanie Southworth, "School Choice and Segregation by Race, Class, and Achievement," in *School Choice:*

Evidence and Recommendations, eds. Gary Miron et al. (Boulder, CO: Education Policy Research Unit and Education and the Public Interest Center, 2008).

7. C. Y. B. Ausbrooks, E. J. Barrett, and T. Daniel, "Texas charter school legislation and the evolution of open-enrollment charter schools," *Education Policy Analysis Archives* 13, no. 21 (2005).

8. Shawna Grosskopf, Kathy J. Hayes, and Lori L. Taylor, "The Relative Efficiency of Charter Schools," *Annals of Public and Cooperative Economics* 80, no. 1 (2009).

9. M. DeArmond, B. Gross, and D. Goldhaber, "Look familiar? Charters and teachers" (Seattle: Center on Reinventing Public Education, 2007), 43–51; Yatsko, Gross, and Christensen, "Alternative paths to graduation"; Cecilia Sam, Joanna Smith, and Priscilla Wohlstetter, "Involving Teachers in Charter School Governance" (Washington, DC: National Resource Center on Charter School Finance and Governance, 2008); Mitch Price, "Still negotiating: What do unions mean for charter schools?" (Seattle: Center on Reinventing Public Education, 2010).

10. For further information, see Sam, Smith, and Wohlstetter, "Involving teachers"; Center on Educational Governance, "Empowering teachers through a CMO-created union: Promising Practices Compendium," National Resource Center on Charter School Finance and Governance, www.charterresource.org (2007).

11. Robin J. Lake and Paul T. Hill, eds. *Hopes, fears & reality: A balanced look at American charter schools in 2009* (Seattle: Center on Reinventing Public Education, 2010).

12. Marisa Cannata, "Teacher Community in Elementary Charter Schools," *Education Policy Analysis Archives* 15, no. 11 (2007); DeArmond, Gross, and Goldhaber, "Look familiar?"; Anthony Milanowski, "The varieties of knowledge and skill-based pay design: A comparison of seven new pay systems for K–12 teachers," *Education Policy Analysis Archives* 11, no. 4 (2003): 1–40; Sam, Smith, and Wohlstetter, "Involving teachers."

13. Marisa Cannata, "Teacher Qualifications and Work Environments Across School Types," in *School Choice: Evidence and Recommendations*, ed. Gary Miron et al. (Boulder, CO: Education Policy Research Unit and Education and the Public Interest Center, 2008).

14. Sam, Smith, and Wohlstetter, "Involving teachers," 11.

15. Yatsko, Gross, and Christensen, "Alternative paths to graduation."

16. Malloy and Wohlstetter, "Working conditions"; Babette M. Benken and Nancy Brown, "Moving beyond the Barriers: A Re-defined, Multi-leveled Partnership Approach to Mathematics Teacher Education," *Issues in Teacher Education* 17, no. 2 (2008); Michael Mintrom, "Market organizations and deliberative democracy: Choice and voice in public service delivery," *Administration & Society* 35, no. 1 (2003).

17. Malloy and Wohlstetter, "Working conditions," 235.

18. Marytza A. Gawlik, "Beyond the charter schoolhouse door: Teacher-perceived autonomy," *Education and Urban Society* 39, no. 4 (2007).

19. Ibid.

20. James Crawford, "Teacher autonomy and accountability in charter schools," *Education and Urban Society* 33, no. 2 (2001).

21. Patricia L. Marshall, Drena C. Gibbs, and Tammy M. Greene, "Teachers reflect on charter schools," *Kappa Delta Pi Record* 37, no. 3 (2001).

22. Sam, Smith, and Wohlstetter, "Involving teachers."

23. Mintrom, "Market organizations."

24. Margolis, "'Every day I spin these plates,'" 87–109; J. Margolis, "Teaching in an urban charter school: stories of success, shadows, and shackles," *Charter School Review* 1, no. 1 (2005): 18–26.

25. Finnigan, "Charter school autonomy"; Malloy and Wohlstetter, "Working conditions"; Steven Adamowski, Susan Bowles Therriault, and Anthony P. Cavanna, "The autonomy gap: Barriers to effective school leadership" (Washington, DC: American Institutes for Research and Thomas B. Fordham Foundation, 2007).

26. Ron Zimmer and Richard Buddin, "Getting inside the black box: Examining how the operation of charter schools affects performance," *Peabody Journal of Education* 82, no. 2–3 (2007); Adamowski, Therriault, and Cavana, "The autonomy gap."

27. Zimmer and Buddin, "Getting inside the black box."

28. Adamowski, Therriault, and Cavana, "The autonomy gap."

29. Ibid.

30. Marytza A. Gawlik, "Breaking Loose: Principal Autonomy in Charter and Public Schools," *Educational Policy* 22, no. 6 (2008).

31. Adamowski, Therriault, and Cavana, "The autonomy gap"; Lawrence F. Garrison and Mitchell Holifield, "Are charter schools effective?," *Planning and Changing* 36, no. 1/2 (2005).

32. Christiana Stoddard and Peter Kuhn, "Incentives and Effort in the Public Sector: Have US Education Reforms Increased Teachers' Work Hours?," *Economics of Education Review* 27, no. 1 (2008); Bruce D. Baker and Jill L. Dickerson, "Charter schools, teacher labor market deregulation, and teacher quality: Evidence from the Schools and Staffing Survey," *Educational Policy* 20, no. 5 (2006).

33. Laura Cumings and Chris L. S. Coryn, "A job analysis for K–8 principals in a nationwide charter school system," *Journal of MultiDisciplinary Evaluation* 6, no. 12 (2009): 157–76.

34. Stephen Jacobson, Lauri Johnson, Rose Ylimaki, and Corrie Giles, "Sustaining success in an American school: A case for governance change," *Journal of Educational Administration* 47, no. 6 (2009).

35. Christine Campbell and Bethany Gross, "Working without a safety net: How charter school leaders can best survive on the high wire" (Seattle: Center on Reinventing Public Education, 2008); Christine Campbell and Brock J. Grubb, "Closing the Skill Gap: New Options for Charter School Leadership Development" (Seattle: Center on Reinventing Public Education, 2008); Laurell Malone and Clarence Davis, "Examining the Landscape of Leadership of Charter School Executives in Low-Performing or Priority Schools in North Carolina," *Academic Leadership* 7, no. 3 (2009).

36. Zimmer and Buddin, "Getting inside the black box."

37. Malone and Davis, "Examining the Landscape."

38. Jacobson, Ylimaki, and Giles, "Sustaining success."

39. John F. Witte, David L. Weiner, Paul A. Schlomer, and Arnold F. Shober,

"The performance of charter schools in Wisconsin," *Journal of Policy Analysis and Management* 26, no. 3 (2007).

40. Richard S. Brown, Priscilla Wohlstetter, and Sunny Liu, "Developing an indicator system for schools of choice: A balanced scorecard approach," *Journal of School Choice* 2, no. 4 (2009): 405.

41. National Resource Center on Charter School Finance and Governance, "Creating and Sustaining High-Quality Charter School Governing Boards," http://www.charterschoolcenter.org/resource/creating-and-sustaining-high-quality-charter-school-governing-boards?; Joanna Smith, Priscilla Wohlstetter, and Dominic Brewer, "Under new management: Are charter schools making the most of new governance options?" (Seattle: Center on Reinventing Public Education, 2007), 17–27.

42. Amy L. Anderson, "The charter school initiative as a case of back to the future," *Educational Foundations* 19, no. 1–2 (2005); Joanna Smith, Chuan Ally Kuzin, Kris De Pedro, and Priscilla Wohlstetter, "Family Engagement in Education, Seven Principles for Success" (Washington, DC: National Resource Center on Charter School Finance and Governance, 2009); Zeng Lin, Dianne C. Gardner, and Paul W. Vogt, "Charter schools in an arena of competitive educational reforms: An analysis of the 1999–2000 schools and staffing survey," *Mid-Western Educational Researcher* 18, no. 2 (2005).

43. National Resource Center on Charter School Finance and Governance, "Creating and Sustaining."

44. Ibid.

45. Christine Campbell, "Missed Opportunity: Improving Charter School Governing Boards," in *Hopes, Fears, and Realities*, ed. Robin Lake (Seattle: Center on Reinventing Public Education, 2007), 59–68.

46. Campbell, "Missed Opportunity."

47. Ibid.

48. Adamowski, Therriault, and Cavana, "The autonomy gap."

49. Zimmer and Buddin, "Getting inside the black box," 264.

50. Finnigan, "Charter school autonomy"; Gawlik, "Breaking Loose"; Gawlik, "Beyond the charter schoolhouse door" (Seattle: Center on Reinventing Public Education, 2009).

51. Also see Priscilla Wohlstetter and Derrick Chau, "Does autonomy matter? Implementing research-based practices in charter and other public schools," in *Taking Account of Charter Schools: What's Happened and What's Next?*, eds. Katrina Bulkley and Priscilla Wohlstetter (New York: Teachers College Press, 2004).

52. Finnigan, "Charter school autonomy."

53. See National Association of Charter School Authorizers, "Principles and Standards for Quality Charter School Authorizing," https://www.qualitycharters.org/policy/principles-and-standards.

54. Christina A. Samuels, "Fulton District Becomes Largest Charter System in Georgia," *Education Week* 31, no. 32 (2012): 8.

CHAPTER FIVE

1. Ellen B. Goldring and Rina Shapira, "Choice, Empowerment, and Involvement:

What Satisfies Parents?" *Educational Evaluation and Policy Analysis* 15, no. 4 (1993).

2. Tennessee, *Tennessee Code Annotated*, "Tennessee Public Charter Schools Act" (2002) § 49-13-102A6.

3. Utah, *Utah Code Annotated*, "State System of Public Education" (1998) § 53A-1A-503.

4. Patricia H. Manz, John W. Fantuzzo, and Thomas J. Power, "Multidimensional assessment of family involvement among urban elementary students," *Journal of School Psychology* 42, no. 6 (2004): 461–75; Christine Waanders, Julia Mendez, and Jason T. Downer, "Parents characteristics, economic stress and neighborhood context as predictors of parent involvement in preschool children's education," *Journal of School Psychology* 45, no. 6 (2007): 619–36.

5. Concha Delgado-Gaitan, "'Consejos': The power of cultural narrative," *Anthropology & Education Quarterly* 25, no. 3 (1994); Laura Desimone, "Linking Parent Involvement with Student Achievement: Do Race and Income Matter?" *Journal of Educational Research* 93, no. 1 (1999).

6. The SEED School, "Student Life," June 28, 2012, www.seedschooldc.org.

7. Wendy Miedel Barnard, "Parent involvement in elementary school and educational attainment," *Children and Youth Services Review* 26, no. 1 (2004): 39–62; Anne T. Henderson and Karen L. Mapp, "A new wave of evidence: The impact of school, family, and community connections on student achievement," in *Annual Synthesis 2002* (Austin, TX: Southwest Educational Development Lab, 2002); Joyce L. Epstein, *School, Family, and Community Partnerships: Preparing Education and Improving Schools* (Boulder, CO: Westview Press, 2001); Xitao Fan and Michael Chen, "Parental Involvement and Students' Academic Achievement: A Meta-Analysis," *Educational Psychology Review* 13, no. 1 (2001); William H. Jeynes, "The Relationship Between Parental Involvement and Urban Secondary School Student Academic Achievement: A Meta-Analysis," *Urban Education* 42, no.1 (2007): 82–110; William H. Jeynes, "A meta-analysis: The effects of parental involvement on minority children's academic achievement," *Education and Urban Society* 35, no. 2 (2003); Jung-Sook Lee and Natasha K. Bowen, "Parent Involvement, Cultural Capital, and the Achievement Gap Among Elementary School Children," *American Education Research Journal* 43, no. 2 (2006): 193–218.

8. Nan Marie Astone and Sara S. McLanahan, "Family structure, parental practices and high school completion," *American Sociological Review* 56, no. 3 (1991): 309–20; Edward J. Cancio, Richard P. West, and K. Richard Young, "Improving mathematics homework completion and accuracy of students with EBD through self-management and parent perception," *Journal of Emotional and Behavioral Disorders* 12, no. 1 (2004): 9–22; Eric Dearing, Kathleen McCartney, Heather B. Weiss, Holly Kreider, and Sandra Simpkins, "The promotive effects of family educational involvement for low-income children's literacy," *Journal of School Psychology* 42, no. 6 (2004): 445–60; Charles V. Izzo, Roger P. Weissberg, Wesley J. Kasprow, and Michael Fendrich, "A longitudinal assessment of teacher perceptions of parent involvement in children's education and school performance," *American Journal of Community Psychology* 27 (1999): 817–39; Leslie Morrison Gutman and Carol Midgley, "The

role of protective factors in supporting the academic achievement of poor African American students during the middle school transition," *Journal of Youth and Adolescence* 29, no. 2 (2000): 233–48; Monique Sénéchal and Jo-Anne LeFevre, "Parental involvement in the development of children's reading skill: A five-year longitudinal study," *Child Development* 73, no. 2 (2002): 445–60; Steven B. Sheldon, "Linking school-family-community partnerships in urban elementary schools to student achievement on state tests," *Urban Review* 35, no. 2 (2003): 149–65.

9. Russell W. Rumberger, "Dropping out of middle school: A multilevel analysis of students and schools," *American Educational Research Journal* 32, no. 3 (1995): 583–625; Wendy T. Miedel and Arthur J. Reynolds, "Parent involvement in early intervention for disadvantaged children: Does it matter?," *Journal of School Psychology* 37, no. 4 (1999): 379–402.

10. Jeynes, "Relationship"; Jeynes, "Effects"; Fan and Chen, "Parental Involvement."

11. Esther Ho Sui-Chu and J. Douglas Willms, "Effects of Parental Involvement on Eighth-Grade Achievement," *Sociology of Education* 69, no. 2 (1996); Frances L. Van Voorhis, "Interactive homework in middle school: Effect on family involvement and students' science achievement," *Journal of Educational Research* 96 (2003); Melissa Ingram, Randi Wolfe, and Joyce Lieberman, "The Role of Parents in High-Achieving Schools Serving Low-Income, At-Risk Populations," *Education and Urban Society* 39, no. 4 (2007).

12. Kathleen V. Hoover-Dempsey, Otto C. Bassler, and Jane S Brissie, "Parent involvement: Contribution to teacher efficacy, school socioeconomic status, and other school characteristics," *American Educational Research Journal* 24, no. 3 (1987); Lee and Bowen, "Parent Involvement, Cultural Capital."

13. Gene H. Brody, Douglas L. Flor, and Nicole Morgan Gibson, "Linking maternal efficacy beliefs, developmental goals, parenting practices and child competence in rural single-parent African American families," *Child Development* 70, no. 5 (1999): 1197–1208.

14. Thomas R. Kratochwill, Lynn McDonald, Joel R. Levin, Holly YoungBear-Tibbets, Michelle K. Demaray, "Families and schools together: An experimental analysis of a parent-mediated multi-family group program for American Indian children," *Journal of School Psychology* 42, no. 5 (2004): 359–83.

15. Christine McWayne and Marissa Owsianik, "A multivariate examination of parent involvement and the social and academic competencies of urban kindergarten children," *Psychology in the Schools* 41, no. 3 (2004): 363–77; Nancy Hill, Domini Castellino, Jennifer Lansford, Patrick Nowlin, Kenneth Dodge, John Bates, and Gregory Petit, "Parent Academic Involvement as Related to School Behavior, Achievement, and Aspirations: Demographic Variations Across Adolescence," *Child Development* 75, no. 5 (2004).

16. Ron Zimmer and Richard Buddin, "Getting inside the black box: Examining how the operation of charter schools affects performance," *Peabody Journal of Education* 82, no. 2–3 (2007).

17. Michael Mintrom, "Market organizations and deliberative democracy: Choice and voice in public service delivery," *Administration & Society* 35, no. 1 (2003).

18. Ibid.

19. A. L. Anderson, "The charter school initiative as a case of back to the future," *Educational Foundations* 19, no. 1–2 (2005); J. Smith, C. Kuzin, Priscilla Wohlstetter, and K. De Pedro, "Parental involvement in urban charter schools: New strategies for increasing participation," *School Community Journal* 21, no. 1 (2011): 71–94; Mintrom, "Market organizations"; Z. Lin, D. C. Gardner, and W. P. Vogt, "Charter schools in an arena of competitive educational reforms: An analysis of the 1999–2000 schools and staffing survey," *Mid-Western Educational Researcher* 18, no. 2 (2005).

20. Lin, Gardner, and Vogt, "Charter schools in an arena."

21. E. K. Davenport and Y. K. H. Bogan, "It takes a village to teach a child: An analysis of an African-centered parent involvement program," *AASA Journal of Scholarship and Practice* 2, no. 3 (2005).

22. Smith, Kuzin, Wohlstetter, and De Pedro, "Parental involvement in urban charter schools"; Davenport and Bogan, "It takes a village."

23. Lin, Gardner, and Vogt, "Charter schools in an arena."

24. Mintrom, "Market organizations."

25. Smith, Kuzin, Wohlstetter, and De Pedro, "Parental involvement in urban charter schools."

26. David R. Garcia, "The Impact of School Choice on Racial Segregation in Charter Schools," *Educational Policy* 22, no. 6 (2008); Christopher Lubienski, "Marketing schools: Consumer goods and competitive incentives for consumer information," *Education and Urban Society* 40, no. 1 (2007); Mark Schneider and Jack Buckley, "What Do Parents Want from Schools? Evidence from the Internet," *Educational Evaluation and Policy Analysis* 24, no. 2 (2002); Natalie Lacireno-Paquet, "Do EMO-operated Charter Schools Serve Disadvantaged Students? The Influence of State Policies" *Education Policy Analysis Archives* 12, no. 26 (2004); Natalie Lacireno-Paquet, "Charter School Enrollments in Context: An Exploration of Organization and Policy Influences," *Peabody Journal of Education* 81, no. 1 (2006); Roslyn Arlin Mickelson, Martha Bottia, and Stephanie Southworth, "School Choice and Segregation by Race, Class, and Achievement," in *School Choice: Evidence and Recommendations*, eds. Gary Miron et al. (Boulder, CO: Education Policy Research Unit and Education and the Public Interest Center, 2008); Paul Teske, Jody Fitzpatrick, and Tracey O'Brien, "Drivers of choice: Parents, transportation, and school choice," ed. Center on Reinventing Public Education (Seattle: Center on Reinventing Public Education, 2009); Carrie Ausbrooks, "Ensuring that underrepresented student groups have access to charter schools: What states are doing," *Planning and Changing* 33, no. 3–4 (2002): 185–96; L. H. Quach, "A paradox of care: [Re]examining education for students with diverse needs," *Educational Foundations* 19, no. 1–2 (2005); Kimberly A. Goyette, "Race, social background, and school choice options," *Equity & Excellence in Education – Special Issue: Class In Education* 41, no. 1 (2008); J. M. Cowen, D. J. Fleming, and A. Gofen, "Measuring the motivation to charter: An examination of school sponsors in Texas," *Journal of School Choice* 2, no. 2 (2008): 301–15.

CHAPTER SIX

1. Jane L. David, "The Who, What, and Why of Site-Based Management,"

Educational Leadership 53, no. 4 (1995): 4–9; Priscilla Wohlstetter and Allan Odden, "Rethinking School-Based Management Policy and Research," *Educational Administration Quarterly* 28, no. 4 (1992): 529–49.

2. Indiana, "Indiana Statutes" (2001) IN Code § 20-24-1-1 to § 20-24-11-4.

3. California, "California Charter Schools Act Part 26.8 of the California Education Code" (1992) Education Code § 47600 to § 47664.

4. Florida, "Florida Statutes" (1996) FL Stat § 1002.33, § 1002.335, § 1002.34, FL Stat § 1013.62.

5. For further information on accountability types, see Brian Stecher and Sheila Nataraj Kirby, "Organizational improvement and accountability: Lessons for education from other sectors" (Santa Monica, CA: Rand Corporation, 2004); Linda Darling-Hammond and Carol Ascher, "Creating Accountability in Big City Schools," Urban Diversity Series No. 102 (New York: National Center for Restructuring Education, Schools and Teaching, 1991); Fred M. Newmann, M. Bruce King, and Mark Rigdon, "Accountability and School Performance: Implications from Restructuring Schools," *Harvard Educational Review* 67, no. 1 (1997): 41–69.

6. Katrina E. Bulkley, "Educational performance and charter school authorizers: The accountability bind," *Education Policy Analysis Archives* 9, no. 37 (2001); Gregg Garn and Casey Cobb, "School Choice and Accountability," in *School Choice: Evidence and Recommendations*, eds. Gary Miron et al. (Boulder, CO: Education Policy Research Unit and Education and the Public Interest Center, 2008); K. Bulkley and J. Fisler, "A decade of charter schools: From theory to practice," *Educational Policy* 17 no. 3 (2003): 317–42; Margaret J. McLaughlin and Lauren Morando Rhim, "Accountability Frameworks and Children with Disabilities: A Test of Assumptions about Improving Public Education for All Students," *International Journal of Disability, Development and Education* 54, no. 1 (2007); Gregg Garn and Casey D. Cobb, "A framework for understanding charter school accountability," *Education and Urban Society* 33, no. 2 (2001); J. M. Cowen, D. J. Fleming, and A. Gofen, "Measuring the motivation to charter: An examination of school sponsors in Texas," *Journal of School Choice* 2, no. 2 (2008): 301–15.

7. Garn and Cobb, "Framework for understanding."

8. Bulkley and Fisler, "Decade of charter schools"; McLaughlin and Rhim, "Accountability Frameworks"; Garn and Cobb, "Framework for understanding."

9. Alison Consoletti, "The State of Charter Schools: What We Do Know—and What We Do Not—About Performance and Accountability" (Washington, DC: The Center for Education Reform, 2011).

10. Louann Bierlein Palmer and Rebecca Gau, "Charter School Authorizing: Policy Implications from a National Study," *Phi Delta Kappan* 86, no. 5 (2005).

11. Ibid, 355.

12. Ibid.

13. Louann Bierlein Palmer, "The Potential of 'Alternative' Charter School Authorizers," *Phi Delta Kappan* 89, no. 4 (2007).

14. Bulkley, "Educational performance"; Carol Ascher and Arthur R. Greenberg, "Charter Reform and the Education Bureaucracy: Lessons from New York State," *Phi Delta Kappan* 83, no. 7 (2002); Public Impact and WestEd, "Supporting Charter

School Excellence Through Quality Authorizing," in *Innovations in Education* (Washington, DC: U.S. Department of Education, 2007); Cheryl M. Lange, Lauren Morando Rhim, and Eileen M. Ahearn, "Special Education in Charter Schools: The View from State Education Agencies," *Journal of Special Education Leadership* 21, no. 1 (2008).

15. Public Impact and WestEd, "Supporting Charter School Excellence," 9.

16. Bulkley, "Educational performance," 7.

17. Public Impact and WestEd, "Supporting Charter School Excellence."

18. Bulkley, "Educational performance."

19. Palmer and Gau, "Charter School Authorizing"; Sandra Vergari, "The regulatory styles of statewide charter school authorizers: Arizona, Massachusetts, and Michigan," *Educational Administration Quarterly* 36, no. 5 (2000): 730–57.

20. Lange, Rhim, and Ahearn, "Special Education."

21. Bulkley, "Educational performance."

22. Vergari, "Regulatory styles," 752.

23. Bulkley, "Educational performance," 11.

24. Palmer and Gau, "Charter School Authorizing," 354.

25. Bulkley, "Educational performance"; Vergari, "Regulatory styles."

26. Vergari, "Regulatory styles."

27. Ibid.

28. Palmer, "Potential of 'Alternative'"; Palmer and Gau, "Charter School Authorizing."

29. Public Impact and WestEd, "Supporting Charter School Excellence," 9.

30. Anna M. Phillips, "New York City Charter School Finds that a Grade of 'C' Means Closing," *New York Times*, January 11, 2012.

31. Noelle C. Griffin and Priscilla Wohlstetter, "Building a plane while flying it: Early lessons from developing charter schools," *Teachers College Record* 103, no. 2 (2001); Roslyn Arlin Mickelson, Martha Bottia, and Stephanie Southworth, "School Choice and Segregation by Race, Class, and Achievement," in *School Choice: Evidence and Recommendations*, eds. Gary Miron et al. (Boulder, CO: Education Policy Research Unit and Education and the Public Interest Center, 2008).

32. Griffin and Wohlstetter, "Building a plane"; Jason M. Barr, Alan R. Sadovnik, and Louisa Visconti, "Charter schools and urban education improvement: A comparison of Newark's district and charter schools," *Urban Review* 38, no. 4 (2006); R. Bifulco and H. F. Ladd, "Results from the Tar Heel state: Older students did better when in regular public schools," *Education Next* 5, no. 4 (2005); Ron Zimmer et al., "Charter schools in eight states: Effects on achievement, attainment, integration, and competition" (Santa Monica, CA: RAND Corporation, 2009); Center for Research on Education Outcomes, "Fact vs. fiction: An analysis of Dr. Hoxby's misrepresentation of CREDO's Research" (Stanford, CA: CREDO, 2009); J. R. Betts and Y. E. Tang, "Value-added and experimental studies on the effects of charter schools on student achievement" (Seattle: Center on Reinventing Public Education, 2008); Jon Christensen, Jacqueline Meijer-Irons, and Robin Lake, "The charter landscape in 2009: The last five years of charter school growth," in *Hopes, Fears and Reality: A Balanced Look at American Charter Schools in 2009*, ed. Robin

Lake (Seattle: Center on Reinventing Public Education, 2009).

33. Betts and Tang, "Value-added and experimental studies."

34. K. S. Finnigan, "Charter school autonomy: The mismatch between theory and practice," *Educational Policy* 21, no. 3 (2007); Katrina E. Bulkley and Jennifer Hicks, "Managing community: Professional community in charter schools operated by educational management organizations," *Educational Administration Quarterly* 41, no. 2 (2005); S. Adamowski, Susan Bowles Therriault, and A. P. Cavana, "The autonomy gap: Barriers to effective school leadership" (Washington, DC: American Institutes for Research and Thomas B. Fordham Foundation, 2007); Arnold F. Shober, Paul Manna, and John F. Witte, "Flexibility Meets Accountability: State Charter School Laws and Their Influence on the Formation of Charter Schools in the United States," *Policy Studies Journal* 34, no. 4 (2006); Paul T. Hill and Jon Christensen, "Safety and order in charter and traditional public schools" (Seattle: Center on Reinventing Public Education, 2007).

35. Bulkley and Hicks, "Managing community," 342.

36. Garn and Cobb, "Framework for understanding."

37. Ibid.; Christopher Lubienski, "Innovation in education markets: Theory and evidence on the impact of competition and choice in charter schools," *American Educational Research Journal* 40, no. 2 (2003); Sara Thuele Lubienski and Christopher Lubienski, "School sector and academic achievement: A multilevel analysis of NAEP mathematics data," *American Educational Research Journal* 43, no. 3 (2006): 651–98.

38. Garn and Cobb, "Framework for understanding."

CHAPTER SEVEN

1. See Daniel Weiler, A Public School Voucher Demonstration: The First Year at Alum Rock, Summary and Conclusions (Santa Monica, CA: The RAND Corporation, 1974).

2. See National Conference of State Legislature, "Education Program: Publicly Funded School Voucher Program," http://www.ncsl.org/issues-research/educ/school-choice-vouchers.aspx.

3. Priscilla Wohlstetter, Noelle Griffin, and Derrick Chau, "Charter schools in California: bruising campaign for public school choice," in *The charter school landscape: Politics, policies, and prospects*, ed. S. Vergari (Pittsburgh: University of Pittsburgh Press, 2002).

4. Eric Rofes, "How are school districts responding to charter laws and charter schools? A Study of Eight States and the District of Columbia" (Berkeley: Policy Analysis for California Education, 1998).

5. National Alliance for Public Charter Schools, A Growing Movement: America's Largest Charter School Communities, 6th ed. (Washington, DC: NAPCS, 2011).

6. Marisa Cannata, "Charter Schools and the Teacher Job Search," *Journal of School Choice* 5, no. 1 (2011): 1.

7. K. Bulkley and J. Fisler, "A decade of charter schools: From theory to practice," *Educational Policy* 17, no. 3 (2003): 317–42.

8. Ibid, 337.

9. George M. Holmes, Jeff DeSimone, and Nicholas G. Rupp, "Friendly Competition," *Education Next* 6, no. 1 (2006); Christiana Stoddard and Peter Kuhn, "Incentives and Effort in the Public Sector: Have US Education Reforms Increased Teachers' Work Hours?," *Economics of Education Review* 27, no. 1 (2008); Matthew Ladner, "The Impact of Charter Schools on Catholic Schools: A Comparison of Programs in Arizona and Michigan," *Catholic Education* 11, no. 1 (2007); Kevin Booker, Scott Gilpatric, Timothy Gronberg, and Dennis Jansen, "The effect of charter schools on traditional public school students in Texas: Are children who stay behind left behind?" *Journal of Urban Economics* 64, no. 1 (2008); John Bohte, "Examining the impact of charter schools on performance in traditional public schools," *Policy Studies Journal* 32, no. 4 (2004).

10. Stoddard and Kuhn, "Incentives and Effort."

11. Ladner, "Impact of Charter Schools."

12. Booker et al., "Effect of charter schools."

13. Bohte, "Examining the impact."

14. Ibid, 516.

15. Ron Zimmer et al., "Evaluating the performance of Philadelphia's charter schools" (Santa Monica, CA: RAND Corporation, 2008); Stéphane Lavertu and John Witte, "The impact of Milwaukee charter schools on student achievement," in *Issues in Governance Studies* (Washington, DC: The Brookings Institute, 2009); Ron Zimmer et al., "Charter schools in eight states: Effects on achievement, attainment, integration, and competition" (Santa Monica, CA: RAND Corporation, 2009); R. Bifulco and H. F. Ladd, "Results from the Tar Heel state: Older students did better when in regular public schools," *Education Next* 5, no. 4 (2005).

16. R. Bifulco and H. F. Ladd, "Institutional Change and Coproduction of Public Services: The Effect of Charter Schools on Parental Involvement," *Journal of Public Administration Research and Theory* 16, no. 4 (2006); Michael L. Marlow, "The influence of private school enrollment on public school performance," *Applied Economics* 42, no. 1 (2010): 11–22; Matthew Carr and Gary Ritter, "Measuring the Competitive Effect of Charter Schools on Student Achievement in Ohio's Traditional Public Schools" (Fayetteville, AR: University of Arkansas, 2007); Yongmei Ni, "The Impact of Charter Schools on the Efficiency of Traditional Public Schools: Evidence from Michigan," *Economics of Education Review* 28, no. 5 (2009).

17. Bifulco and Ladd, "Institutional Change."

18. Ni, "Impact of Charter Schools."

19. Carr and Ritter, "Measuring the Competitive Effect."

20. David Arsen and Yongmei Ni, "The Competitive Effect of School Choice Policies on Performance in Traditional Public Schools," in *School Choice: Evidence and Recommendations*, eds. Gary Miron et al. (Boulder, CO: Education Policy Research Unit and Education and the Public Interest Center, 2008).

21. Ibid, 12.

22. Scott A. Imberman, "The Effect of Charter Schools on Non-Charter Students: An Instrumental Variables Approach" (Houston, TX: National Center for the Study of Privatization in Education, 2007).

23. Arsen and Ni, "Competitive Effect of School Choice Policies," 12.

24. Bulkley and Fisler, "Decade of charter schools," 336.

25. Stoddard and Kuhn, "Incentives and Effort."

26. Frederick Hess, Robert Maranto, and Scott Milliman, "Small districts in big trouble: How four Arizona school systems responded to charter competition," *Teachers College Record* 103, no. 6 (2001): 1107.

27. Judy J. May, "The Market-Driven Age of Education: Challenges of Urban School Leadership," *Mid-Western Educational Researcher* 20, no. 4 (2007).

28. Ibid, 32.

29. Richard Buddin and Ron Zimmer, "Is Charter School Competition in California Improving the Performance of Traditional Public Schools?" *Public Administration Review* 69, no. 5 (2009).

30. Rita G. O'Sullivan, Barry Nagle, Kelly Spence, and Chris Haynes, "First year's impact of North Carolina's charter schools on local school districts (LEAs)," *The High School Journal* 83, no. 4 (2000).

31. Joe Nathan and William L. Boyd, "Lessons about School Choice from Minnesota: Promise and Challenges," *Phi Delta Kappan* 84, no. 5 (2003): 351.

32. Linda A. Renzulli, "Organizational Environments and the Emergence of Charter Schools in the U.S.," *Sociology of Education* 78, no. 1 (2005): 18.

33. S. Grosskopf, K. Hayes, and L. Taylor, "The Relative Efficiency of Charter Schools," *Annals of Public and Cooperative Economics* 80, no. 1 (2009).

34. Cynthia Hill and David Welsch, "For-profit versus not-for-profit charter schools: An examination of Michigan student test scores," *Education Economics* 17, no. 2 (2009).

35. Stuart S. Yeh, "The Cost-Effectiveness of Five Policies for Improving Student Achievement," *American Journal of Evaluation* 28, no. 4 (2007).

36. Zimmer and Buddin, "Charter School Competition in California," 835.

37. See Katrina Bulkley, Jeffrey R. Henig, and Henry Levin, *Between Public and Private: Politics, Governance and the New Portfolio Models for Urban School Reform* (Cambridge, MA: Harvard Education Press, 2010).

38. Douglas Lee Lauen, "To Choose or Not to Choose: High School Choice and Graduation in Chicago," *Educational Evaluation & Policy Analysis* 31, no. 3 (2009).

39. Gary Wolfram, "Effect of Time Spent in Charter Schools on Student Test Scores: A Michigan Case Study" (presented at San Diego, CA: Western Economic Association Meetings, 2006).

40. Imberman, "Effect of Charter Schools," 27.

41. Bill and Melinda Gates Foundation, "Gates foundation announces significant investments available for cities supporting collaboration, bold reform and high-performing schools," December 6, 2011, http://www.gatesfoundation.org/press-releases/Pages/high-performing-school-investments-111206.aspx.

42. "Editorial: New compact offers a truce in charter wars," *Sacramento Bee*, April 9, 2012, http://www.sacbee.com/2012/04/09/4399763/new-compact-offers-a-truce-in.html.

43. NYC Collaborates, "NYC Collaborates: Committed to students. Inspired to share," June 30, 2012, www.nyccollaborates.org.

44. Ed Finkel, "District-Charter Collaborations on the Rise," http://www.districtadministration.com/article/district-charter-collaborations-rise.

45. Philadelphia School Partnership, "About Us," www.philaschoolpartnership.org.

46. YES Prep, "YES Prep to Partner with KIPP and Spring Branch ISD in SKY Partnership," December 8, 2011, http://yesprep.org/TheAnswer/full/press_release_yes_prep_to_partner_with_kipp_and_spring_branch_isd_in_sky_pa/

CHAPTER EIGHT

1. Sandra Vergari, ed., *The Charter School Landscape* (Pittsburgh: University of Pittsburgh Press, 2002).

2. Carrie Ausbrooks, "Ensuring That Underrepresented Student Groups Have Access to Charter Schools: What States Are Doing," *Planning & Changing* 33, no. 3–4 (2002): 191.

3. Pauline Lipman and Nathan Haines, "From accountability to privatization and African American exclusion: Chicago's 'Renaissance 2010,'" *Educational Policy* 21, no. 3 (2007); Natalie Lacireno-Paquet, "Charter School Enrollments in Context: An Exploration of Organization and Policy Influences," *Peabody Journal of Education* 81, no. 1 (2006); Luis Urrieta Jr., "Heritage charter school: A case of conservative local white activism through a postmodern framework," *Educational Foundations* 19, no. 1–2 (2005).

4. Ron Zimmer et al., "Charter schools in eight states: Effects on achievement, attainment, integration, and competition" (Santa Monica, CA: RAND Corporation, 2009); Robert Bifulco and Helen F. Ladd, "School choice, racial segregation, and test-score gaps: Evidence from North Carolina's charter school program," *Journal of Policy Analysis and Management* 26, no. 1 (2007): 31–56; Roslyn Arlin Mickelson, Martha Bottia, and Stephanie Southworth, "School Choice and Segregation by Race, Class, and Achievement," in *School Choice: Evidence and Recommendations*, eds. Gary Miron et al. (Boulder, CO: Education Policy Research Unit and Education and the Public Interest Center, 2008); Ron Zimmer et al., "Evaluating the performance of Philadelphia's charter schools" (Santa Monica, CA: RAND Corporation, 2008).

5. Zimmer et al., "Charter schools in eight states."

6. Mickelson, Bottia, and Southworth, "School Choice."

7. Bifulco and Ladd, "School choice, racial segregation."

8. Urrieta, "Heritage charter school"; Amy Stambach and Natalie Crow Becker, "Finding the old in the new: On race and class in US charter school debates," *Race, Ethnicity and Education* 9, no. 2 (2006); Thomas Dee and Helen Fu, "Do Charter Schools Skim Students or Drain Resources?" *Economics of Educational Review* 23, no. 3 (2003); L. A. Renzulli, "District Segregation, Race Legislation, and Black Enrollment in Charter Schools," *Social Science Quarterly* 87, no. 3 (2006).

9. Renzulli, "District Segregation," 412.

10. Urrieta, "Heritage charter school."

11. Renzulli, "District Segregation."

12. Natalie Lacireno-Paquet and Charleen Brantley, "Who Chooses Schools, and

Why?" (Boulder, CO: Education Policy Research Unit and Education and the Public Interest Center, 2008).

13. D. Garcia, "The Impact of School Choice on Racial Segregation in Charter Schools," *Educational Policy* 22, no. 6 (2008): 805; D. Garcia, "Academic and Racial Segregation in Charter Schools: Do Parents Sort Students into Specialized Charter Schools?" *Education and Urban Society* 40, no. 5 (2008): 590.

14. Bifulco and Ladd, "School choice, racial segregation."

15. Emily Arcia, "A test of the segregation premise," *Journal of School Choice* 1, no. 2 (2006).

16. Kevin Booker, Brian Gill, Ron Zimmer, and Tim Sass, "Achievement and Attainment in Chicago Charter Schools" (Santa Monica, CA: RAND Corporation, 2009); Zimmer et al., "Charter schools in eight states"; Salvatore Saporito and Deenesh Sohoni, "Coloring Outside the Lines: Racial Segregation in Public Schools and Their Attendance Boundaries," *Sociology of Education* 79, no. 2 (2006).

17. Zimmer et al., "Charter schools in eight states."

18. Saporito and Sohoni, "Coloring Outside the Lines."

19. Mickelson, Bottia, and Southworth, "School Choice."

20. Garcia, "Impact of School Choice"; Garcia, "Academic and Racial Segregation."

21. Luis Urrieta, "Community identity discourse and the heritage academy: Color-blind educational policy and white supremacy," *International Journal of Qualitative Studies in Education* 19, no. 4 (2006): 470.

22. Suzanne E. Eckes and Anne E. Trotter, "Are charter schools using recruitment strategies to increase student body diversity?," *Education and Urban Society* 40, no. 1 (2007): 62–90.

23. Kent L. Tedin and Gregory R. Weiher, "Racial/Ethnic diversity and academic quality as components of school choice," *Journal of Politics* 66, no. 4 (2004); Lacireno-Paquet and Brantley, "Who Chooses Schools?"; Suzanne E. Eckes, "Barriers to integration in the Mississippi Delta: Could charter schools be the new vehicle for desegregation?," *Analyses of Social Issues and Public Policy* 6, no. 4 (2006); Stambach and Becker, "Finding the old in the new"; Mickelson, Bottia, and Southworth, "School Choice"; Gregory R. Weiher and Kent L. Tedin, "Does choice lead to racially distinctive schools? Charter schools and household preferences," *Journal of Policy Analysis and Management* 21, no. 1 (2002); Carrie Y. Barron Ausbrooks, Edith J. Barrett, and Theresa Daniel, "Texas charter school legislation and the evolution of open-enrollment charter schools," *Education Policy Analysis Archives* 13, no. 21 (2005).

24. Lacireno-Paquet and Brantley, "Who Chooses Schools?"; Mickelson, Bottia, and Southworth, "School Choice"; Weiher and Tedin, "Does choice lead to racially distinctive schools?"; Ausbrooks, Barrett, and Daniel, "Texas charter school legislation."

25. Weiher and Tedin, "Does choice lead to racially distinctive schools?" 82.

26. Bifulco and Ladd, "School choice, racial segregation"; Renzulli, "District Segregation"; Mickelson, Bottia, and Southworth, "School Choice"; Linda A Renzulli and Lorraine Evans, "School choice, charter schools, and white flight," *Social Problems* 52, no. 3 (2005).

27. Bifulco and Ladd, "School choice, racial segregation."

28. Eckes and Trotter, "Are charter schools using recruitment strategies?"

29. Chad d'Entremont and Charisse Gulosino, "Circles of Influence: How Neighborhood Demographics and Charter School Locations Influence Student Enrollment" (New York: National Center for the Study of Privatization in Education, 2008), 18.

30. Mickelson, Bottia, and Southworth, "School Choice," 15.

31. Renzulli and Evans, "School choice, charter schools," 412.

32. Eckes and Trotter, "Are charter schools using recruitment strategies?" 81.

33. Ibid.

34. Arcia, "A test of the segregation premise."

35. Renzulli and Evans, "School choice, charter schools."

36. Tedin and Weiher, "Racial/Ethnic diversity and academic quality."

37. Renzulli and Evans, "School choice, charter schools."

38. Kelly E. Rapp and Suzanne E. Eckes, "Dispelling the Myth of 'White Flight': An Examination of Minority Enrollment in Charter Schools," *Educational Policy* 21, no. 4 (2007): 620.

39. Mickelson, Bottia, and Southworth, "School Choice,"13.

40. Salvatore Saporito and Deenesh Sohoni, "Mapping educational inequality: Concentrations of poverty among poor and minority students in public schools," *Social Forces* 85, no. 3 (2007): 1,238.

41. K. Bulkley and J. Fisler, "A decade of charter schools: From theory to practice," *Educational Policy* 17, no. 3 (2003): 332.

42. Natalie Lacireno-Paquet, Thomas T. Holyoke, Michele Moser, and Jeffrey R. Henig, "Creaming versus Cropping: Charter School Enrollment Practices in Response to Market Incentives," *Educational Evaluation and Policy Analysis* 24, no. 2 (2002).

43. Jeffrey R. Henig, "What Do We Know About the Outcomes of KIPP Schools?" (Boulder, CO: Education Policy Research Unit and Education and the Public Interest Center, 2008).

44. Caroline M. Hoxby, Sonali Murarka, and Jenny Kang, "How New York City's Charter Schools Affect Achievement," in *New York City's Charter Schools Evaluation Project* (New York: New York City, 2009).

45. R. Zimmer et al., "Charter schools in eight states."

46. R. Zimmer, B. Gill, K. Booker, S. Lavertu, and J. Witte, "Examining charter student achievement effects across seven states," *Economics of Education Review* 31, no. 2 (2012): 213–24.

47. Cynthia D. Hill and David M. Welsch, "For-profit versus not-for-profit charter schools: An examination of Michigan student test scores," *Education Economics* 17, no. 2 (2009); Heath Brown, Jeffrey Henig, Natalie Lacireno-Paquet, and Thomas T. Holyoke, "Scale of operations and locus of control in market- versus mission-oriented charter schools," *Social Science Quarterly* 85, no. 5 (2004); Natalie Lacireno-Paquet, "Do EMO-operated Charter Schools Serve Disadvantaged Students? The Influence of State Policies," *Education Policy Analysis Archives* 12, no. 26 (2004); Lacireno-Paquet, "Charter School Enrollments in Context"; T. Holyoke,

"Dimensions of charter school choice," *Journal of School Choice* 2, no. 3 (2008): 302–17; Katrina Bulkley, "Losing Voice?: Educational Management Organizations and Charter Schools' Educational Programs," *Education and Urban Society* 37, no. 2 (2005): 204; Julie Marsh, Laura Hamilton, and Brian Gill, "Assistance and Accountability in Externally Managed Schools: The Case of Edison Schools, Inc," *Peabody Journal of Education* 83, no. 3 (2008); Heath Brown, "Incentives in U.S. charter schools: For-profit and nonprofit choices," *Journal of School Choice* 2, no. 4 (2008): 415–39; J. M. Cowen, D. J. Fleming, and A. Gofen, "Measuring the motivation to charter: An examination of school sponsors in Texas," *Journal of School Choice* 2, no. 2 (2008): 301–15.

48. Marsh, Hamilton, and Gill, "Assistance and Accountability"; G. Wolfram, "Effect of time spent in charter schools on student test scores: A Michigan case study," *Journal of School Choice* 2, no. 1 (2008): 20–46; Steven F. Wilson, Henry Levin, and Jay Mathews, "Realizing the promise of brand-name schools," in *Brookings Papers on Education Policy 2005* (Washington, DC: The Brookings Institution, 2005).

49. C. Lubienski, "Innovation in education markets: Theory and evidence on the impact of competition and choice in charter schools," *American Educational Research Journal* 40, no. 2 (2003); Priscilla Wohlstetter, Richard Wenning, and Kerri L. Briggs, "Charter schools in the United States: The question of autonomy," *Educational Policy* 9, no. 4 (1995).

50. Center for Education Reform, "The accountability report: Charter schools" (Washington, DC: CER, 2009).

51. EdSector, "Growing pains: Scaling up the nation's best charter schools" (Washington, DC: ES, 2009).

52. Bill and Melinda Gates Foundation, "Investment to Accelerate Creation of Strong Charter Schools," www.gatesfoundation.org/press-releases/Pages/newschools-venture-receives-grant-030630.aspx; NewSchools Venture Fund, "Charter management organizations: Toward scale with quality," http://newschools.org/files/CMO-monograph.pdf.

53. Guilbert Hentschke, Jennifer Herman, Joanna Smith, Caitlin C. Farrell, and Priscilla Wohlstetter, "Funding strategies to achieve scale: How charter management organizations finance their growth," in *2010 Annual Meeting of the American Educational Research Association* (Denver: American Educational Research Association, 2010).

54. Joshua Furgeson, "Charter-School Management Organizations: Diverse Strategies and Diverse Student Impacts" (Seattle: Mathematica Policy Research and Center on Reinventing Public Education, 2011).

55. Brian Edwards, Heather Barondess, and Eric Crane, "Spotlight on CMOs: Defining and analyzing charter management organizations" (Mountain View, CA: EdSource, 2009), 24–30.

56. Richard D. Kahlenberg and Halley Potter, "Diverse charter schools: Can racial and socioeconomic integration promote better outcomes for students?" (Washington, DC: The Century Foundation/The Poverty and Race Research Action Council, 2012); Nora Kern, Renita Thukral, and Todd Ziebarth, "A Mission to Serve: How

Public Charter Schools are Designed to Meet the Diverse Demands of Our Communities" (Washington, DC: National Alliance for Public Charter Schools, 2012).

57. Jaclyn Zubrzycki, "Studies Spotlight Charters Designed for Integration," *Education Week* 31, no. 33 (2012): 1, 18–19.

58. Ibid.

CHAPTER NINE

1. Chester Finn Jr., Bruno Manno, and Gregg Vanourek, *Charter Schools in Action* (Princeton, NJ: Princeton University Press, 2001).

2. Ed Finkel, "District-Charter Collaborations on the Rise," *District Administration Magazine*, September 1, 2011.

3. Alex Medler as cited in Ed Finkel, ibid.

4. Finkel, ibid.

5. Caitlin Farrell, Priscilla Wohlstetter, and Joanna Smith, "Charter management organizations: An emerging approach to scaling up what works," *Educational Policy* 26, no. 4 (2012): 499–532; Robin Lake, Brianna Dusseault, Melissa Bowen, Allison Demeritt, and Paul Hill, *The national study of charter management organization (CMO) effectiveness: Report on interim findings* (Seattle: Mathematica Policy Research and Center on Reinventing Public Education, 2010).

CONCLUSION

1. Pushpam Jain, "The Approval Barrier to Suburban Charter Schools" (Washington, DC: Thomas B. Fordham Foundation, 2002): 2.

2. Winnie Hu, "Battle Over Charter Schools Shifting to Affluent Suburbs," *New York Times*, July 16, 2011 (A1).

3. David Stuit and Sy Doan, "Beyond City Limits: Expanding Public Charter Schools in Rural America" (Washington, DC: National Alliance for Public Charter Schools, 2012):10–11.

4. Ibid.

5. William Frey, "Population and Migration," in *The State of Metropolitan America* (Washington, DC: Brookings Institution, 2010): 37–49.

6. Success Academy Charter Schools, "Our Schools," http://mysuccessacademy .org/

7. Joan L. Herman, Jia Wang, Jordan Rickles, Vivian Hsu, Scott Monroe, Seth Leon, and Rolf Straubhaar, "Evaluation of Green Dot's Locke Transformation Project: Findings for Cohort 1 and 2 Students" (Los Angeles: National Center for Research on Evaluations, Standards, and Student Testing, 2012).

8. Julian R. Betts and Y. Emily Tang, "The effect of charter schools on student achievement: A meta-analysis of the literature" (Seattle: Center on Reinventing Public Education, 2011): 3.

9. For example, see Paul Berman and Milbrey Wallin McLaughlin, *Federal Programs Supporting Educational Change,* vol. 1, *A Model of Educational Change* (Santa Monica, CA: RAND Corporation, 1974).

10. Center on Educational Governance, "School Performance Dashboard 2012" (Los Angeles: Center on Educational Governance, 2012).

11. Christopher Lubienski and Charisse A. Gulosino, "Choice, competition, and organizational orientation: A geo-spatial analysis of charter schools and the distribution of educational opportunities" (New York: National Center for the Study of Privatization in Education, 2007); Cathy Krop and Ron Zimmer, "Charter school type matters when considering funding and facilities: Evidence from California," *Education Policy Analysis Archives* 13, no. 50 (2005); Janelle Scott, "The politics of venture philanthropy in charter school policy and advocacy," *Educational Policy* 23, no. 1 (2009): 106–36.

12. Baldrige: Information You Need to Build the Organization You Want, "Baldrige 101" (http://www.baldrige.com/baldrige-process/baldrige-101) and "Customer Focus" (http://www.baldrige.com/criteria_customerfocus/the-three-cs-of-customer-retention-character-community-and-content/).

13. Margaret Raymond, "Multiple Choice: Charter School Performance in 16 States" (Palo Alto, CA: Center for Research on Education Outcomes, 2009).

14. Center on Educational Governance, "School Performance Dashboard 2012."

15. Dick M. Carpenter II, *Playing to Type? Mapping the Charter School Landscape* (Washington, DC: The Thomas B. Fordham Institute, 2005).

APPENDIX

1. Barbara Means, Yukie Toyama, Robert Murphy, Marianne Bakia, and Karla Jones, "Evaluation of Evidence-Based Practices in Online Learning: A Meta-Analysis and Review of Online Learning Studies" (Washington, DC: U.S. Department of Education: Office of Planning, Evaluation, and Policy Development, 2009); Zoe Garrett, Mark Newman, Diane Elbourne, Steve Bradley, Philip Noden, Jim Taylor, and Anne West, "Secondary School Size: A Systematic Review," in *Research Evidence in Education Library* (London, UK: EPPI-Center Social Science Research Unit, Institute of Education University of London, 2004); Anthony Petrosino and Julia Lavenberg, "Systematic reviews and meta-analyses: Best evidence on 'what works' for criminal justice decision makers," *Western Criminology Review* 8, no. 1 (2007); Vincent A. Anfara Jr., Kathleen M. Brown, and Terri L. Mangione, "Qualitative analysis on stage: Making the research process more public," *Educational Researcher* 31, no. 28 (2002).

2. Iain Chalmers and Douglas Altman, *Systematic reviews* (London, UK: BMI, 1995), as cited in Petrosino and Lavenberg, "Systematic reviews."

3. Anfara, Brown, and Mangione, "Qualitative analysis."

4. As identified by PAIS International Peer Reviewed Journals List: http://www.csa.com/factsheets/supplements.paispeer.php.

5. Peter M. Miller, "A Critical Analysis of the Research on Student Homelessness," *Review of Educational Research* 81, no. 3 (2011); Sara Goldrick-Rab, "Challenges and Opportunities for Improving Community College Student Success," *Review of Educational Research* 80, no. 3 (2010); American Educational Research Association, "Standards for Reporting on Empirical Social Science Research in AERA Publications," *Educational Researcher* 35, no. 6 (2006); Michael C. McKenna and Sharon Walpole, "Planning and Evaluation Change at Scale: Lessons from Reading First," *Educational Researcher* 39, no. 6 (2010).

6. American Educational Research Association, "Standards for Reporting."

ACKNOWLEDGMENTS

The U.S. Department of Education provided the initial support that set us off on our journey more than two years ago—a journey that would eventually lead to this book. Early in our travels we worked with Martin Orland of WestEd, who offered feedback on preliminary drafts of our technical report that synthesized a decade of charter school research. With the twentieth anniversary of the charter school movement on the horizon, we turned to Caroline Chauncey, editor in chief and assistant director of Harvard Education Press, to create a wholly new effort focused on examining whether the goals set forth in charter school laws have been borne out in empirical research findings. Caroline lent her wisdom, experience, and skills to the project, and also kept us moving in the right direction and in a timely fashion. By joining us early on in the journey, Caroline provided a psychological boost: she quickly committed to the project and believed in us. We picked up the pace of writing.

Numerous people helped us along the way. The research team from the Center on Educational Governance (CEG) at the University of Southern California (USC) whittled the universe of over seven thousand publications on charter schools down to a relevant five hundred or so. The CEG researchers—students from USC's Dana and David Dornsife College of Letters, Arts and Sciences, and from the Rossier School of Education and the Sol Price School of Public Policy—were, in alphabetical order: Jeimee Estrada, Henry Franco, Michelle Nayfack, Rohini Thukral, and Annette Wong. They were incredibly productive and reliable, and they contributed greatly to the project design and analysis. Paul O'Neill offered us (on extended loan) the CD version of the *Charter School Law Deskbook*—an invaluable tool in our analysis of charter school laws. Cassandra Jackson and Susan Valiza of CEG provided excellent project support and lots of encouragement.

Our faculty colleagues at the Center on Educational Governance, in particular Guilbert Hentschke and Katharine Struck, offered a valuable sounding board—Gib for his thoughtful insights on charter schools and Katharine for her help in digesting the piles of articles and reports on student achievement in charter schools.

In the home stretch, a new group joined us and accelerated our pace to the finish line. Michael Kirst contributed the foreword to the book. Five other distinguished reformers and researchers—Jeff Henig, Paul Hill, Bruno Manno, Deborah McGriff, and Charles Payne—agreed to be interviewed about their personal views of charter schools and the movement looking back and into the future. In the final stage, we also relied heavily on Beatrice Fuchs, a research assistant at CEG. Her attention to detail and her computer competency made all of our work much easier.

Finally, to our partners, Ted, David, and Carlos, who offered unfailing support and tolerated many late nights, we thank you for your encouragement throughout our journey.

ABOUT THE AUTHORS

PRISCILLA WOHLSTETTER is Distinguished Research Professor in the Department of Education Policy and Social Analysis at Teachers College, Columbia University, and a senior research fellow with the Consortium for Policy Research in Education. Prior to joining Teachers College, she was the Diane and MacDonald Becket Professor in Education Policy at the University of Southern California's Rossier School of Education, where she also was founder and director of USC's Center on Educational Governance.

Her research explores the policy and politics of K–12 urban education, as well as the relationship between school governance and improved school performance. She has served as principal investigator for numerous national and international studies focusing on urban reform. She directed a national study of charter schools and public-private partnerships, and served as co-director for the National Resource Center for Charter School Finance and Governance, both funded by the U.S. Department of Education. In partnership with the charter community, she developed a state accountability system for California charter schools (the USC School Performance Dashboard). Her publications include numerous articles on federal and state education policies, local governance, public-private partnerships, and the use of data-driven decision-making to improve school performance. Her books include *Taking Account of Charter Schools* (with Katrina E. Bulkley) and *School-Based Management: Organizing for High Performance* (with Susan A. Mohrman and associates).

Dr. Wohlstetter received her masters in education and social policy from Harvard Graduate School of Education, and her PhD in public policy from Northwestern University. She was awarded a post-doctoral fellowship at RAND upon completing her graduate education.

JOANNA SMITH is an assistant research professor at the University of Southern California's Rossier School of Education and assistant director of the Center on Educational Governance. Dr. Smith received her PhD in educational policy and administration from Rossier in 2004; her dissertation examined partnerships between charter schools and community-based organizations.

Dr. Smith's research utilizes qualitative approaches to study education policy, innovation, and reform. Her work has been published in numerous peer-reviewed journals including *Education Finance and Policy, School Leadership and Management, Policy Studies Journal*, and *Educational Administration Quarterly*. She regularly presents her work at national and state conferences and has coauthored numerous reports, issue briefs, and practitioner-focused guidebooks. Dr. Smith began her career in education as a high school English and ESL teacher at an Islamic school in Melbourne, Australia. She has taught in Rossier's online MAT-TESOL program as well as the EdD program.

CAITLIN C. FARRELL is a postdoctoral fellow at the University of California, Berkeley, where she researches effective partnerships between school districts and research organizations. She holds a PhD in urban education policy from the University of Southern California, where her dissertation focused on comparative analysis of data-use strategies in traditional school districts and charter management organizations.

Dr. Farrell specializes in research on policy implementation, K–12 urban educational reform, and accountability, and her research blends perspectives in education, public policy, and organizational theory. Her prior work on educational governance has been published in *Educational Policy, Journal of Education Finance*, and *Journal of School Choice*. She began her career in education as an elementary school teacher after attending Dartmouth College for her BA and Pace University for a masters in childhood education.

ABOUT THE CONTRIBUTORS

JEFFREY R. HENIG is a professor of political science and education at Teachers College and a professor of political science at Columbia University. He leads and teaches in the Program on Education and Politics at Teachers College and chairs the new policy department, Education Policy and Social Analysis. His scholarly interests include race and urban politics, the politics of urban education reform, and the politics of education research. His many books, which have received recognition from the American Political Science Association and the American Educational Research Association, are written from a political perspective, including *The Color of School Reform: Race, Politics and the Challenge of Urban Education* (1999), *Building Civic Capacity: The Politics of Reforming Urban Schools* (2001), and *Spin Cycle: How Research Is Used in Policy Debates: The Case of Charter Schools* (2008); he has coauthored *Between Public and Private: Politics, Governance, and the New Portfolio Models for Urban School Reform* (2010). Dr. Henig earned his BA at Cornell University in 1973 and his PhD at Northwestern University in 1978.

PAUL T. HILL is founder and former director of the Center on Reinventing Public Education at the University of Washington, Bothell. He is a nonresident senior fellow at the Brookings and Hoover Institutions and directed the National Working Commission on Choice in K–12 Education. Dr. Hill's current work on public education reform focuses on school choice, finance, accountability, and charter schools. His books include *Charter Schools Against the Odds* (2006); *Making School Reform Work: New Partnerships* *for Real Change* (2004); *Charter Schools and Accountability in Public Education* (2002); *It Takes A City: Getting Serious About Urban School Reform* (2000); and *Fixing Urban Schools* (1998). Dr. Hill holds a PhD and MA from Ohio State University and a BA from Seattle University, all in political science.

MICHAEL W. KIRST is professor emeritus of Education and Business Administration at Stanford University. He has been on the Stanford faculty since 1969. In 2011 Kirst became president of the California State Board of Education for the second time, having been a member of the board from 1975 to 1982 and its president from 1977 to 1981. Before joining the Stanford University faculty, Dr. Kirst held several positions with the federal government, including staff director of the U.S. Senate Subcommittee on Employment, Manpower and Poverty, and director of program planning for elementary and secondary education of the U.S. Office of Education. His book *From High School to College*, written with Andrea Venezia, was published in 2004, and in 2009 he coauthored *The Political Dynamics of American Education* with Frederick M. Wirt. Dr. Kirst received his PhD in political economy and government from Harvard University.

BRUNO MANNO is currently senior advisor at the Walton Family Foundation. Before joining the foundation he was senior program associate for education with the Annie E. Casey Foundation, and before that he was senior fellow in the Education Policy Studies Program at the Hudson Institute. During the 1980s he held the position of assistant secretary for policy and planning in the U.S. Department of Education and several other leadership positions in the Office of Educational Research and Improvement under the Reagan administration. He is the coauthor or author of numerous books and articles on K–12 education policy and reform, including one of the first books on charters, *Charter Schools in Action* (2001), with coauthors Chester E. Finn Jr. and Gregg Vanourek. He received a BA and MA from the University of Dayton and a PhD from Boston College.

DEBORAH MCGRIFF is a partner at NewSchools Venture Fund and leads the National Network of Charter Schools to enhance college readiness and success. She began her career with the New York City public schools and stayed there for more than a decade. As she rose through the education system, she served as deputy superintendent in Milwaukee, Wisconsin, and assistant superintendent in Cambridge, Massachusetts. Dr. McGriff finished up her administrative career as superintendent of the Detroit public schools. In the 1990s she joined EdisonLearning, Inc. (formerly Edison Schools), where she held numerous leadership positions, among them the executive vice president of charter schools. She currently serves on the boards of the Policy Innovators in Education Network and the National Alliance for Public Charter Schools, and she is the founder and a national board member of the Black Alliance for Educational Options. Dr. McGriff holds a BA from Norfolk State University, an MA from Queens College of the City University of New York, and a PhD from Fordham University.

CHARLES M. PAYNE is an academic whose areas of study include civil rights activism, urban education reform, social inequality, and modern African American history. He is currently the Frank P. Hixon Distinguished Service Professor at the University of Chicago's School of Social Service Administration, where he is also affiliated with the Urban Education Institute. He has written several books focused on urban education: *Getting What We Ask For: The Ambiguity of Success and Failure in Urban Education* (1984), *So Much Reform, So Little Change* (2008), and *Teach Freedom* (2008). Dr. Payne has also been active in the creation and direction of several organizations intended to address issues of social justice. He is the founding director of the Urban Education Project in Orange, New Jersey, a community-based effort to provide advanced career training for local youth. Dr. Payne received a BA in Afro-American studies from Syracuse University and a PhD in sociology from Northwestern University.

INDEX